Mountain Biking
St. George/
Cedar City

BRUCE GRUBBS

FALCON® Helena, Montana

AFALCONGUIDE®

Falcon® Publishing is continually expanding its list of recreation guidebooks. All books include detailed descriptions, accurate maps, and all the information necessary for enjoyable trips. You can order extra copies of this book and get information and prices for other Falcon® guidebooks by writing Falcon, P.O. Box 1718, Helena, MT 59624 or calling toll free 1-800-582-2665. Also, please ask for a free copy of our current catalog. Visit our website at www.FalconOutdoors.com

©1999 Falcon® Publishing, Inc., Helena, Montana.
Printed in Canada.

1 2 3 4 5 6 7 8 9 0 TP 04 03 02 01 00 99

Falcon and FalconGuide are registered trademarks of Falcon® Publishing, Inc.

Cover photo by Howie Garber.

Library of Congress Cataloging-in-Publication Data

Grubbs, Bruce (Bruce O.)
    Mountain biking St. George/Cedar City / Bruce Grubbs.
        p.   cm. — (A Falcon guide)
    Includes index.
    ISBN 1-56044-803-2 (pbk. : alk. paper)
    1. All terrain cycling—Utah—Saint George Region—Guidebooks.
    2. All terrain cycling—Utah—Cedar City Region—Guidebooks.
    3. Bicycle trails—Utah—Saint George Region—Guidebooks.
    4. Bicycle trails—Utah—Cedar City Region—Guidebooks.   5. Saint
    George Region (Utah)—Guidebooks.   6. Cedar City Region (Utah)—
    Guidebooks.   I. Title.   II. Title: St. George/Cedar City.
    III. Title: Mountain biking Saint George/Cedar City.   IV. Series.
    GV1045.4.U82S354   1998
    796.6'3'0979247—dc21   98-48431
                                                              CIP

CAUTION

Outdoor recreational activities are by their very nature potentially hazardous. All participants in such activities must assume the responsibility for their own actions and safety. The information contained in this guidebook cannot replace sound judgment and good decision-making skills, which help reduce risk exposure, nor does the scope of this book allow for disclosure of all the potential hazards and risks involved in such activities.

   Learn as much as possible about the outdoor recreational activities in which you participate, prepare for the unexpected, and be cautious. The reward will be a safer and more enjoyable experience.

 Text pages printed on recycled paper.

Contents

Acknowledgments v
Map Legend vi
Overview Map vii

Get Ready to CRANK!
The St. George/Cedar City Area: What to Expect 2
IMBA Rules of the Trail 6
How to Use this Guide 8
Elevation Graphs 13
The Name Game 14

St. George
1   Pine Valley Loop 15
2   Gunlock Loop 18
3   West Canyon 21
4   Green Valley Loop 24
5   Stucki Spring Loop 28
6   Church Rocks Loop 32
7   Warner Valley 35
8   Dutchman Trail 39
9   Silver Reef 42
10   Oak Grove 45

Zion
11   J.E.M. Trail 48
12   Gooseberry Mesa 52
13   Grafton 57

Cedar City
14   Red Mountain 60
15   Blowhard Mountain 63
16   Cedar Breaks 66
17   Navajo Lake Loop 69
18   Cascade Falls Loop 72
19   Ice Cave Loop 76
20   Strawberry Point Loop 79

MAP LEGEND

Trail		Trailhead	
Unimproved Road		Route Marker	
Paved Road		Elevation/Peak	
Gravel Road		Interstate	15
Interstate		U.S. Highway	12
Wilderness Boundary		State Highway/County Road	143
Waterway		Forest Road	092
Lake/Reservoir		Gate	
Cliff		Building	
Camping		Scale/Compass	

N

0   1   2   3

MILES

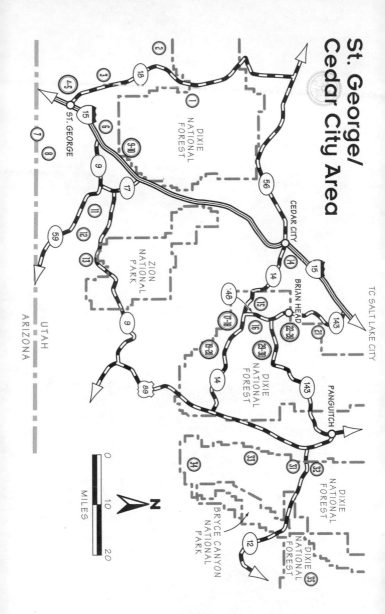

St. George/Cedar City Area

Get Ready to CRANK!

Where to ride? It's a quandary that faces every mountain biker, beginner or expert, local or tourist.

If you're new to the area, where do you start? If you're a long-time local, how do you avoid the rut of riding the same old trails week after week? And how do you find new terrain that's challenging but not overwhelming? Or an easier ride for when you're not-so-serious buddies come along?

Welcome to *Mountain Biking St. George/Cedar City*. Here are 35 rides ranging from easy road routes to smooth singletrack to challenging, technical slickrock. The rides are described in plain language, with accurate distances and ratings for physical and technical difficulty. Each entry offers a wealth of detailed information that's easy to read and use, from an armchair or on the trail.

My aim is threefold: to help you choose a ride that's appropriate for your fitness and skill level; to make it easy to find the trailhead; and to help you complete the ride safely, without getting lost. Take care of those basics and fun is bound to break loose.

some of the rides. The newer editions have a long-awaited topographic base—but use caution, the contours are in meters while the spot elevations are in feet. The USGS topos and other useful maps are listed for each ride. Finally—I'll say it again—always wear a helmet.

The **weather** in Utah's Color Country spans the range of North American extremes. On the high plateaus at Brian Head and Bryce, snow can fall any month of the year. Summer highs routinely top 100 degrees F in St. George. In general, higher elevations are cooler (by as much as 10 degrees F for every 1,000 feet) and windier. If you drive to a trailhead, play it safe and take a variety of clothes in the car to match the weather you're likely to encounter. Drink extra fluids while driving to "prehydrate"; even in cool weather, the humidity is usually low.

Riding **seasons** depend mostly on elevation. During winter, the best riding is found near St. George. During spring, St. George is still good, but the Zion and Cedar City areas also dry out then. Summer is very hot in the low desert (below 4,000 feet), so desert riders prefer to ride at first light, or at night with lights. By mid-May, the Bryce area (at 8,000 feet) is normally dry and rideable, as are many of the rides east of Cedar City. Brian Head, the highest area, at 11,000 feet, is usually snow free by mid-June. During fall, the riding is glorious at Brian Head as the aspens change to shades of yellow and gold, but early mornings are cold. The first snows may fall in October at the highest elevations, but nearly all the routes in this book are rideable during fall. (Bear in mind that hunting seasons may occur during good riding weather. Check with the Utah State Division of Wildlife Resources for current hunting seasons; see the Appendix. If you choose to ride during hunting season, a blaze-orange vest is a sensible precaution.)

Afternoon thunderstorms are common during July, August, and September. These storms can appear suddenly and are often severe, with hail, high wind, and lightning. If caught in a thunderstorm, get off the high ridges and take shelter in a low-lying area or in a vehicle. Do not remain under lone trees. During thunderstorm season, the mornings generally dawn sweet and clear, the air refreshed by yesterday's showers. It's a good idea to complete your day's riding by noon. Please stay off wet, muddy trails—the soil damage and erosion one rider can cause is simply too severe.

The high plateaus attract more rain and snow than do the desert valleys around St. George and Cedar City. The low deserts get some snow in the winter, but it usually melts on the first clear day. Many of the desert rides dry out after one day of sun. The rides in this book vary in base elevation from 2,500 feet to over 11,000 feet, which means you can ride dirt all year, somewhere in Color Country.

The cities and towns in the area covered by this guide (St. George, Hurricane, Springdale, Cedar City, Brian Head, and Panguitch) have a large variety of visitor services, including motels, restaurants, stores, gas stations, public and private campgrounds, and bike shops. These establishments are far too numerous to mention here, but I have included a list of area bike shops in the Appendix. It's a good idea to check with the nearest bike shop before setting out on a ride; the locals have the latest information on trail conditions.

Campgrounds and motels tend to fill up early during the tourist season, especially near the national parks and monuments, so you might want to make reservations. As an alternative to designated campgrounds, camping is generally allowed in national forests and on public lands administered by the Bureau of Land Management or the State of Utah, unless otherwise posted. Remember that inholdings of private land are found in national forests and other public lands; respect all no-trespassing signs unless you have permission from the landowner.

IMBA Rules of the Trail

If every mountain biker always yielded the right-of-way, stayed on the trail, avoided wet or muddy trails, never cut switchbacks, always rode in control, showed respect for other trail users, and carried out every last scrap of what was carried in (candy wrappers and bike-part debris included)—in short, if we all *did the right thing*—we wouldn't need a list of rules governing our behavior.

Fact is, most mountain bikers are conscientious and are trying to do the right thing. No one becomes good at something as demanding and painful as grunting up mountainsides by cheating. Most of us don't need rules.

But we do need knowledge of what exactly is the right thing to do. Thousands of miles of dirt trails have been closed to mountain bicyclists. The irresponsible riding habits of a few riders have been a factor. Do your part to maintain trail access by observing the following rules of the trail, formulated by the International Mountain Bicycling Association (IMBA). IMBA's mission is to promote environmentally sound and socially responsible mountain biking.

Here are some guidelines, reprinted with permission from the IMBA. The basic idea is to prevent or minimize damage to land, water, plants, and wildlife, and to avoid conflicts with other backcountry visitors and trail users. Ride with respect.

1. Ride on open trails only. Respect trail and road closures (ask if not sure), avoid possible trespass on private land, obtain permits and authorization as may be required. Federal and state wilderness areas are closed to cycling. The way you ride will influence trail management decisions and policies.

2. Leave no trace. Be sensitive to the dirt beneath you. Even on open (legal) trails, you should not ride under conditions where you will leave evidence of your passing, such as on certain soils after a rain. Recognize different types of soils and trail construction; practice low-impact cycling. This also means staying on existing trails and not creating new ones. Be sure to pack out at least as much as you pack in.

3. Control your bicycle! Inattention for even a second can cause problems. Obey all bicycle speed regulations and recommendations.

4. Always yield trail. Make known your approach well in advance. A friendly greeting (or bell) is considerate and works well; don't startle others. Show your respect when passing by slowing to a walking pace or stopping. Anticipate other trail users at corners and blind spots.

5. Never spook animals. An unannounced approach, a sudden movement, or a loud noise startles all animals. This can be dangerous for you, others, and the animals. Give animals extra room and time to adjust to you. When passing horses, use special care and follow directions from the horseback riders (dismount and ask if uncertain). Chasing cattle and disturbing wildlife are serious offenses. Leave gates as you found them, or as marked.

6. Plan ahead. Know your equipment, your ability, and the area in which you are riding—and prepare accordingly. Be self-sufficient at all times, keep your equipment in good repair, and carry necessary supplies for changes in weather or other conditions. A well-executed trip is a satisfaction to you and not a burden or offense to others. Always wear a helmet.

Keep trails open by setting a good example of environmentally sound and socially responsible off-road cycling.

How to Use this Guide

Mountain Biking St. George/Cedar City describes 35 mountain bike rides in their entirety. Many of the featured rides are loops, beginning and ending at the same point but coming and going on different trails. Loops are by far the most popular type of ride, and we're lucky to have so many in the St. George/Cedar City area.

Be forewarned, however: the difficulty of a loop may change dramatically depending on which direction you ride around the loop. If you are unfamiliar with the rides in this book, try them first as described here. The directions follow the path of least resistance and most fun (which does not necessarily mean easy). After you've been over the terrain, you can determine whether a given loop would be fun—or even feasible—in the reverse direction.

Portions of some rides follow gravel or even paved roads, and there's one ride that's all road. Purists may wince at road rides in a book about mountain biking, but this one is special.

Each ride description follows the same format:

Number: Rides are cross referenced by number throughout this book. In many cases, parts of rides or entire routes can be linked to other rides for longer rides or variations on a standard route. These opportunities are noted, followed by "see Ride(s) #."

Name: For the most part, I relied on official names of trails, roads, and natural features as shown on USDA Forest Service and U.S. Geological Survey maps. In some cases deference was given to long-term local custom.

Location: The general whereabouts of the ride; distance and direction from St. George, Springdale, Cedar City, Brian Head, or Panguitch.

Distance: The length of the ride in miles, given as a loop, one way, or out and back.

Time: A conservative estimate of how long it takes to complete the ride, for example, 1 to 2 hours. *The time listed is the actual riding time and does not include rest stops*. Strong, skilled riders may be able to do a given ride in less than the estimated time, while other riders may take considerably longer. Also bear in mind that severe weather, changes in trail conditions, or mechanical problems may prolong a ride.

Tread: The type of road or trail surface—paved road, maintained dirt road, doubletrack, ATV-width singletrack, or singletrack.

Aerobic level: The level of physical effort required to complete the ride: rated as easy, moderate, or strenuous.

Easy: Flat or gently rolling terrain. No steep or prolonged climbs.

Moderate: Some hills. Climbs may be short and fairly steep or long and gradual. There may be short hills that less fit riders will want to walk.

Strenuous: Frequent or prolonged climbs steep enough to require riding in the lowest gear; requires a high level of aerobic fitness, power, and endurance (typically acquired through many hours of riding and proper training). Less fit riders may need to walk.

Many rides are mostly easy and moderate but may have short strenuous sections. Other rides are mostly strenuous and should be attempted only after a complete medical checkup and implant of a second heart, preferably a big one. Also, be aware that flailing through a highly technical section can be exhausting even on the flats. Good riding skills and a relaxed stance on the bike save energy.

Finally, any ride can be strenuous, especially at higher elevations, if you ride it hard and fast. Conversely, the pain of a lung-burning climb grows easier to tolerate as your fitness level improves. Learn to pace yourself and remember to schedule easy rides and rest days into your calendar.

Technical difficulty: The level of bike handling skills needed to complete the ride upright and in one piece. Technical difficulty is rated on a scale of 1 to 5, with 1 being the easiest and 5 the hardest.

Level 1: Smooth tread; road or doubletrack; no obstacles, ruts, or steeps. Requires basic bike-handling skills.

Level 2: Mostly smooth tread; wide, well-groomed singletrack or road/doubletrack with minor ruts or loose gravel or sand.

Level 3: Irregular tread with some rough sections; slickrock, single- or doubletrack with obvious route choices; some steep sections; occasional obstacles may include small rocks, roots, water bars, ruts, loose gravel or sand, and sharp turns or broad, open switchbacks.

Level 4: Rough tread with few smooth places; singletrack or rough doubletrack with limited route choices; steep sections, some with obstacles; obstacles are numerous and varied, including rocks, roots, branches, ruts, sidehills, narrow tread, loose gravel or sand, and switchbacks. Most slickrock is rated level 4.

Level 5: Continuously broken, rocky, root-infested, or trenched tread; singletrack or extremely rough doubletrack with few route choices; frequent, sudden, and severe changes in gradient; some slopes so steep that wheels lift off ground; obstacles are nearly continuous and may include boulders, logs, water, large holes, deep ruts, ledges, piles of loose gravel, steep sidehills, encroaching trees, and tight switchbacks.

I've also added plus (+) and minus (-) symbols to cover gray areas between given levels of difficulty; a 4+ obstacle is harder than a 4, but easier than a -5. A stretch of trail rated as 5+ would be unrideable by all but the most skilled riders.

Again, most of the rides in this book cover varied terrain, with an ever-changing degree of technical difficulty. Some trails run smooth with only occasional obstacles, and other trails are seemingly all obstacle. The path of least resistance, or line, is where you find it. In general, most obstacles are more challenging if you encounter them while climbing than while descending. On the other hand, in heavy surf (e.g., boulder fields, tangles of downfall, cliffs), fear plays a larger role when facing downhill.

Realize, too, that different riders have different strengths and weaknesses. Some folks can scramble over logs and boulders without a grunt, but they crash head over heels on every switchback turn. Some fly off the steepest slopes and others freeze. Some riders climb like the wind and others just blow… and walk.

The key to overcoming "technical difficulties" is practice: keep trying. Follow a rider who makes it look easy, and don't hesitate to ask for constructive criticism. Try shifting your weight (good riders move a lot, front to back, side to side, and up and down) and experimenting with balance and momentum. Find a smooth patch of lawn and practice riding as slowly as possible, even balancing in a track stand (described in the Glossary). This will give you more confidence—and more time to recover or bail out—the next time the trail rears up and bites.

Hazards: A list of dangers that may be encountered on a ride, including traffic, weather, trail obstacles and conditions, risky stream crossings, obscure trails, and other perils. Remember that conditions may change at any time. Be alert for storms, flash floods, new fences, deadfall, missing trail signs, mechanical failure, rattlesnakes, scorpions, spiny plants, and cliff edges. Fatigue, heat, cold, and/or dehydration may impair judgment. Always wear a helmet and other safety equipment. Ride in control at all times.

Highlights: Special features or qualities that make a ride worth doing (as if we needed an excuse!) such as scenery, fun singletrack, or chances to see wildlife.

Land status: A list of managing agencies or land owners. Most of the rides in this book are in the Dixie National Forest or land administered by the Bureau of Land Management. But many of the rides also cross portions of private, state, county, or municipal lands. Always leave gates as you found them, or as signed, and respect the land and property, regardless of who owns it. See the Appendix for a list of local addresses for land management agencies.

Maps: A list of available maps. The two Dixie National Forest maps covering the Pine Valley and Cedar City ranger districts, and the Powell, Escalante, and Teasdale ranger districts at a scale of 1:126,720 afford a good overview of travel routes in the area. Several maps published by Trails Illustrated are useful. USGS topographic maps in the 7.5-minute quadrangle series give a close-up look at terrain. The USGS 1:100,000 metric topographic series (St. George, Cedar City, and Panguitch) give a topographic overview. Not all routes are shown on official maps.

Access: How to find the trailhead or the start of the ride. Some rides can be pedaled right from the nearest town; for others you'll have to drive to the trailhead.

The ride: A mile-by-mile list of key points—landmarks, notable climbs and descents, stream crossings, obstacles, hazards, major turns and junctions—along the ride. All distances were measured to the hundredth of a mile (they were rounded to the nearest tenth for the listing) with a carefully calibrated cyclometer. As a result, you will find a cyclometer to be very useful for following the descriptions. Trails were carefully mapped using the USGS 7.5-minute topographic maps as a reference. A Global Positioning System (GPS) receiver was used to supplement more traditional methods of land navigation where landmarks were obscure. Terrain, riding technique, and even tire pressure can affect odometer readings, so treat all mileages as estimates.

Finally, one last reminder that the real world is changing all the time. The information presented here is as accurate and up-to-date as possible, but there are no guarantees out in the backcountry. You alone are responsible for your safety and for the choices you make on the trail. Contact the nearest bike shop or the appropriate land management agency for the latest trail information. See the Appendix for addresses and phone numbers.

If you do find an error or omission in this book, or a new and noteworthy change in a ride, I'd like to hear from you. Please write to Bruce Grubbs, c/o Falcon Publishing, P.O. Box 1718, Helena, Montana 59624.

Elevation Graphs

An elevation profile accompanies each ride description. Here the ups and downs of the route are graphed on a grid of elevation (in feet above sea level) on the left and miles pedaled across the bottom. Route surface conditions (see map legend), and technical levels are shown on the graphs.

Note that these graphs are compressed (squeezed) to fit on the page. The actual slopes you will ride are not as steep as the lines drawn on the graphs (it just feels that way). Also, some extremely short dips and climbs are too small to show up on

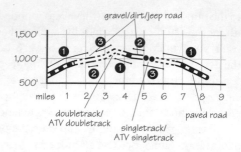

the graphs. All such abrupt changes in gradient are, however, mentioned in the mile-by-mile ride description.

The Name Game

Mountain bikers often assign their own descriptive nicknames to trails. These nicknames may help distinguish or describe certain parts of the overall ride, but only for the group of people that knows the nickname. All too often, the nicknames are meaningless—or misleading—to cyclists who haven't spun their pedals on the weekly group ride.

For the sake of clarity, I stuck to the official (or at least most widely accepted) names for the trails and roads described in this book. When a route is commonly known by more than one name, the other names are mentioned. If you know them by some other name, or if you come up with nicknames that peg the personalities of these rides, then by all means share them with your riding buddies.

Pine Valley Loop

Location: About 25 miles north of St. George.

Distance: 33.9-mile loop.

Time: 5 hours.

Tread: 19.6 miles on maintained dirt road; 14.3 miles on paved road.

Aerobic level: Moderate.

Technical difficulty: 2 on dirt road; 1 on paved roads.

Hazards: A few rutted areas on the dirt roads. This ride is muddy when wet; wait a day after rain for it to dry out.

Highlights: Scenic loop through Pine and Grass valleys, with optional historic sites.

Land status: Dixie National Forest; private.

Maps: USGS Central East, Central West, Enterprise, Pinto, Page Ranch, Grass Valley; Dixie National Forest (Pine Valley and Cedar City ranger districts).

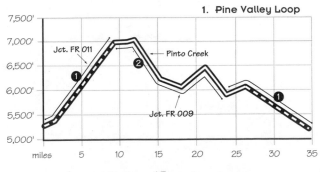

1. Pine Valley Loop

● Pine Valley Loop

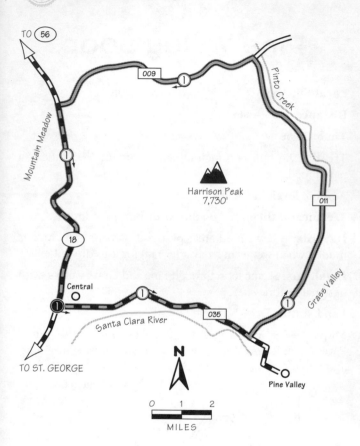

TO 56

Mountain Meadow

009

1

1

18

Harrison Peak
7,730'

Pinto Creek

011

Central
O

1

1

035

Grass Valley

Santa Clara River

TO ST. GEORGE

O
Pine Valley

N

0   1   2

MILES

Access: From St. George, drive north on Utah Highway 18 about 25 miles to the Central and Pine Valley turnoff (Forest Road 035), and park.

The Ride

0.0 Ride east on the paved road to Pine Valley. The road climbs gradually toward the Pine Valley Mountains, visible ahead.

1.5 Pass the Dixie National Forest boundary.

7.0 Turn left on Pinto Road (Forest Road 011). This maintained dirt road climbs steadily north.

9.3 Roll down into Grass Valley, a broad meadow.

10.9 Now start a gradual climb out of Grass Valley.

11.8 You've reached the top of the climb. Start a moderate descent into the South Fork Pinto Creek drainage.

15.5 The descent becomes gentler.

18.3 Go left at the T intersection with FR 009. This maintained dirt road climbs gradually to the west.

21.3 Ride over a pass and start a moderate descent.

26.6 Hang a left on UT 18, and roll south across Mountain Meadow.

33.9 Pine Valley turnoff, and the end of the ride.

Gunlock Loop

Location: About 21 miles north of St. George.

Distance: 18.2-mile loop.

Time: 4 hours.

Tread: 9.8 miles on paved road; 8.4 miles on maintained dirt road.

Aerobic level: Moderate.

Technical difficulty: 1 on paved roads; 2 on dirt roads.

Hazards: Watch for traffic on the paved road as well as some ruts on the dirt road, depending on weather and maintenance. The dirt portion of the ride should be avoided for a day after heavy rain; it becomes icky mud.

Highlights: Easy, scenic loop ride with no technical sections. The entire loop is a good ride for beginners who are in decent shape. With a car shuttle, the dirt road can be done as a one-way, mostly downhill ride, which is suitable for nearly anyone.

Land status: Bureau of Land Management; private.

Maps: USGS Gunlock, Veyo.

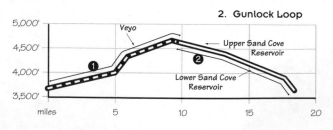

•Gunlock Loop

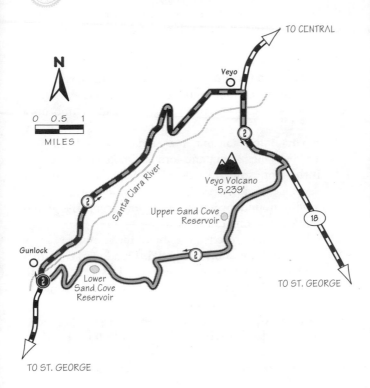

Access: From St. George, drive north on Utah Highway 18 (Bluff Street), then turn left on Sunset Boulevard, toward Santa Clara. After 12 miles, turn right on the paved road to Gunlock Reservoir. Continue 9 miles, past the reservoir, and park near the bridge at the south end of Gunlock. To do the dirt section of the ride one way with a shuttle, leave a vehicle here and follow the ride directions below to mile 9.8 to shuttle the second vehicle to the start of the dirt road.

19

The Ride

0.0   Pedal across the bridge and through the town of Gunlock. The paved road follows the scenic Santa Clara River valley to the northeast.

2.0   Crank up a short climb.

2.5   Coast down the other side. The road roller coasters up and down as it follows the narrow river valley.

5.1   Swing right as the road starts a steady climb up a switchback, away from the river.

5.9   Top out onto a volcanic mesa and cruise west. The scenic Pine Valley Mountains form an impressive backdrop.

7.7   Turn right (south) onto UT 18 in the little town of Veyo. Coast down a hill, across a bridge, then climb steadily around the left side of Veyo Volcano, the prominent cinder cone to the south.

9.2   Whew! You've reached the top of the climb.

9.8   Hang a right on a maintained dirt road marked with a BLM sign for Sand Cove Reservoirs. This is the point to start the ride if you're doing a car shuttle from Gunlock. It's almost all downhill from here.

11.4   Ride past Upper Sand Cove Reservoirs.

13.3   Start a moderate descent. Watch for ruts if the road was recently wet.

14.5   The road levels out as you ride past an electrical substation.

15.5   Pedal up a short climb.

15.7   Roll down past Lower Sand Cove Reservoir.

17.0   While cruising along this sage flat, you have good views of the cliffs of Red Mountain to the left.

17.3   Start a steep descent to Gunlock.

17.8   After a switchback, you'll be at the bottom of the descent in the Santa Clara River valley.

18.2   Welcome back to Gunlock, the river bridge, and the end of the ride.

West Canyon

Location: About 10 miles north of St. George.

Distance: 7.6 miles out and back.

Time: 1 hour.

Tread: 7.6 miles on maintained dirt road.

Aerobic level: Easy.

Technical difficulty: 2 on wide singletrack.

Hazards: Occasional washouts at gully crossings. Watch for horses on the road and at trail crossings.

Highlights: An easy ride on a smooth, wide singletrack through a spectacular sandstone canyon in Snow Canyon State Park. The road is closed to all but authorized motor vehicles, which makes it especially pleasant. This is an excellent choice for beginning riders and family groups. More physically fit riders can ride this trail from St. George.

Land status: State of Utah.

Maps: USGS Santa Clara.

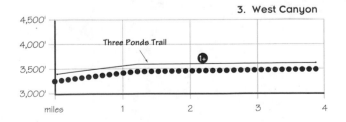

•West Canyon

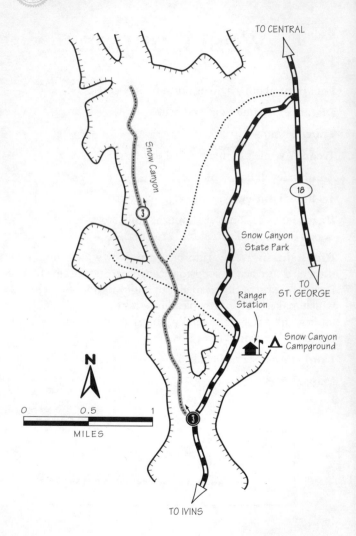

TO CENTRAL

Snow Canyon

3

18

Snow Canyon
State Park

Ranger
Station

TO
ST. GEORGE

Snow Canyon
Campground

N

0   0.5   1

MILES

3

TO IVINS

22

Access: From St. George, drive north on Utah Highway 18 (Bluff Street) about 10 miles, then turn left at the sign for Snow Canyon State Park. After 2 miles, stop at the ranger station for a day-use permit ($4 per vehicle as of this writing). The trailhead is a large gravel parking lot and picnic area on the right, 0.6 mile past the ranger station.

The Ride

0.0   Ride north around the gate on the narrow gravel road. There are a few slight descents along the way, but the trail generally climbs as it heads up West Canyon.

1.1   A horse trail crosses the road.

1.2   The Three Ponds Trail goes left 1.5 miles to the ponds. This is an optional side hike; if you plan to do this, bring a bike lock.

1.8   Another horse trail goes right.

3.8   End of the ride at the head of the canyon. Take a break and enjoy the silence of this steep-walled, box canyon before starting the easy roll back to the trailhead.

Green Valley Loop

Location: About 6 miles west of St. George.

Distance: 10.2-mile loop (10.7 miles with the optional return).

Time: 2 hours.

Tread: 3.8 miles on singletrack; 4.6 miles on doubletrack; 1.8 miles on paved road. The optional return has the same amount of singletrack; 1.4 miles on doubletrack; and 5.5 miles on paved road.

Aerobic level: Moderate.

Technical difficulty: 3+ on singletrack; 2 with sections of 2+ on doubletrack; 1 on paved roads.

Hazards: Several steep descents on the singletrack, sometimes with little warning; rocks and ruts on doubletrack; traffic on main paved roads.

Highlights: Also known as Bloomington Loop, this is a popular trail with a fun, swooping, roller-coaster stretch of singletrack.

Land status: Bureau of Land Management; private.

Maps: USGS White Hills, St. George.

Access: From St. George, at St. George Boulevard and Interstate 15, drive 1.9 miles west on St. George Boulevard, then turn left on Bluff Street. After 1.8 miles, turn right on Hilton Drive, just before the I-15 intersection. Go 1.5 miles, then turn right on Dixie Drive (just past the golf course). Go 2 miles, turn left on

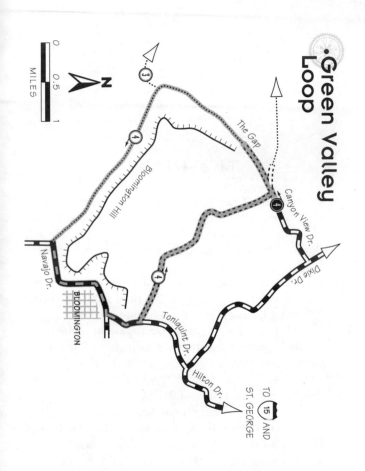

Green Valley Loop

The Gap

Bloomington Hill

Canyon View Dr.

Dixie Dr.

Toniquint Dr.

Navajo Dr.

BLOOMINGTON

Hilton Dr.

TO 15 AND ST. GEORGE

N

MILES
0 0.5 1

Canyon View Drive, then go 0.7 mile to the end of the pavement. Park in the broad area at the edge of the bluff, straight ahead.

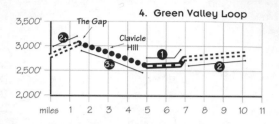

The Ride

0.0   From the trailhead, look southwest across the valley at the Gap, a notch in the ridge. Note the doubletrack climbing along the right (west) side of this notch; ride down off the bluff and make your way through the confusion of roads and trails to that doubletrack.

0.4   Pass through a wire gate and start climbing the moderate grade. Generally, stay to the right at intersections, following the most heavily used route.

1.4   Pedal through a wire gate at the top of the climb. Note the trail visible in the distance, swinging left below the bluffs of Bloomington Hill. The trail becomes singletrack, traverses left, and drops steeply into a wash via several choices of various difficulty.

2.0   Ride out of the wash on the left. From here until it reaches pavement, the singletrack follows the base of Bloomington Hill. Numerous ATV trails branch right; stay left at all intersections to remain on the bike trail.

2.8   Ride or walk down the steep descent known as Clavicle Hill (for the numerous collarbone-crunching crashes it produces). After this, begin the fun roller-coaster section—watch for sudden changes in direction, abrupt drops, and multiple trail choices.

4.6   Cross under a powerline.

5.2   Go through a gate, across a cattleguard, and onto paved Navajo Drive.

5.6   As you roll through the residential area, don't miss the petroglyphs at Petroglyph Park, on the left.

5.7   Hang a left on Bloomington Drive.

6.6   Do another left onto Toniquint Drive, and grunt up a short steep hill.

7.0   Turn left onto the powerline road, a moderately rocky doubletrack. For an alternate return on the paved streets that is 0.5 mile longer but takes less time, see below.

7.5   The climb moderates as you pass a fence.

7.8   Ride left, to stay with the powerline.

8.0   Pedal right; you still want to follow the powerline.

8.4   The faithful powerline Ts into another powerline; go right, downhill.

8.6   Another gate, which, of course, you should leave as you found it.

8.9   The road veers left and descends into the valley you crossed at the beginning of the ride.

9.3   Go through yet another wire gate, then bear generally right to reach the trailhead.

10.2 Trailhead.

Paved Return Option: At the powerline on Toniquint Drive, continue on the paved road.

8.0   Turn left on Dixie Drive.

10.0 Turn left again on Canyon View Drive.

10.7 Trailhead.

Stucki Spring Loop

Location: About 6 miles west of St. George.

Distance: 12.3-mile loop.

Time: 2.5 hours.

Tread: 9.8 miles on singletrack; 2.5 miles on doubletrack.

Aerobic level: Moderate.

Technical difficulty: 3+ on singletrack; 2 and 3 on doubletrack.

Hazards: Several sudden, steep descents; be alert for ATVs on parts of the trail. The trail will be muddy after a rain, so allow a day for it to dry out.

Highlights: Lots of fun, roller-coaster singletrack, with great views thrown in.

Land status: Bureau of Land Management; private.

Maps: USGS White Hills, St. George.

Access: From St. George, at St. George Boulevard and Interstate 15, drive 1.9 miles west on St. George Boulevard, then turn left on Bluff Street. After 1.8 miles, turn right on Hilton Drive, just before the I-15 intersection. Go 1.5 miles, then turn right on Dixie Drive (just past the golf course). Go 2 miles, turn left on Canyon View Drive, then go 0.7 mile to the end of the pavement. Park in the broad area at the edge of the bluff, straight ahead.

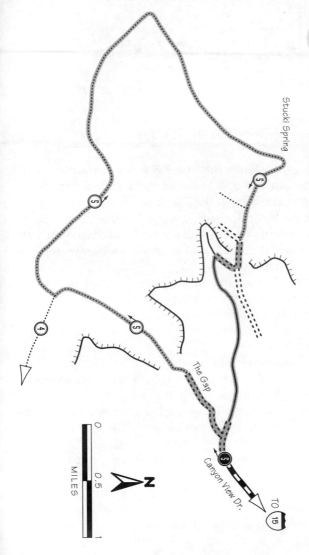

•Stucki Spring Loop

Stucki Spring

The Gap

Canyon View Dr.

TO 15

MILES
0   0.5   1

N

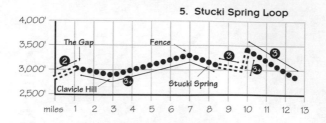

The Ride

0.0 This ride shares the first 2.8 miles of trail with the Green Valley Loop. From the trailhead, look southwest across the valley at the Gap, a notch in the ridge. Note the doubletrack climbing along the right (west) side of this notch; ride down off the bluff and make your way through the confusion of roads and trails to that doubletrack.

0.4 Go through a wire gate and start climbing, staying on the trail that shows the most use.

1.4 Go through another wire gate at the top of the climb. The trail becomes singletrack and drops steeply into a wash.

2.0 Ride out of the wash on the left.

2.8 Ride or walk down Clavicle Hill, then turn sharply right on singletrack that descends southwest.

2.9 Turn right again on singletrack that follows an old road. The trail winds over ridges and hills, but generally heads west and climbs gradually in a roller-coaster fashion. Ride the most heavily used trail and you'll stay on track.

6.8 Ride up to a fence, which marks the top of the climb. The previous part of the ride has been along the top of a bluff, and the high point offers a great view of the surrounding hills. Turning toward the northeast, the trail now does a series of roller coasters, following the faint remnant of a straight bulldozer track.

8.4 Bear right at a fork in the singletrack (the most heavily used trail).

8.6 A water tank marks Stucki Spring. Pedal right at a T intersection with an ATV trail. Note the steep doubletrack climbing the bluff to the east; that is your goal.

9.5 A doubletrack merges from the right.

9.7 Start the steep but short climb to the top of the bluff.

9.8 Turn right and crank uphill on the rocky doubletrack along the edge of the bluff.

10.0 Turn sharply left on singletrack marked with a cairn, and start a fun downhill cruise. The trailhead is visible on the bluff a couple of miles ahead.

11.8 Bounce over a short rocky area, after which the trail becomes doubletrack.

11.9 Go left and through the wire gate, then up the bluff to the trailhead.

12.3 Trailhead.

Option: Many locals prefer to reverse the loop. It's fun either way. For a longer ride, ride Stucki Spring in reverse, then finish by joining the Green Valley Loop at the base of Clavicle Hill. The combined trails are 17.3 miles.

Church Rocks Loop

Location: About 6 miles northeast of St. George.

Distance: 6.4-mile loop, with a cherry stem (see Glossary).

Time: 2 hours.

Tread: 3 miles on singletrack; 3.4 miles on maintained dirt.

Aerobic level: Moderate.

Technical difficulty: 3+ on singletrack; 1 on maintained dirt road.

Hazards: Watch for a few dropoffs and a short steep section.

Highlights: The singletrack is nearly all slickrock. This easily accessible ride is a fine introduction to slickrock, and the views are great too!

Land status: Bureau of Land Management; state of Utah.

Maps: USGS Harrisburg Junction.

Access: From St. George, drive northeast on Interstate 15 and exit at Washington. Turn right onto Green Springs Drive, then left on Telegraph Street. At the top of a short, steep hill about 6 miles from St. George, turn left on an unmarked, maintained dirt road and park. Local riders often start this ride from I-15 via the Washington exit, or from St. George via Red Cliffs Drive.

•Church Rocks Loop

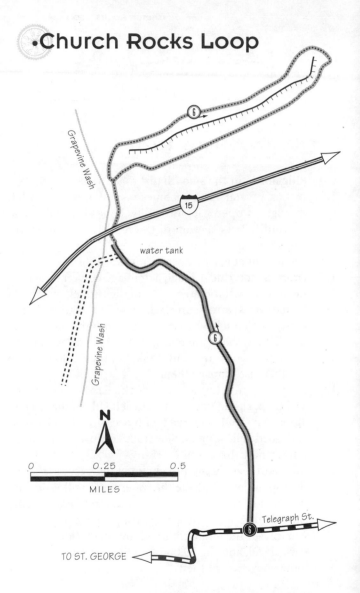

Grapevine Wash

6

15

water tank

6

Grapevine Wash

N

0   0.25   0.5

MILES

6   Telegraph St.

TO ST. GEORGE

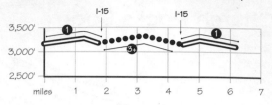

6. Church Rocks Loop

The Ride

0.0 Ride north on the smooth dirt road, toward I-15.

1.3 Just as a water tank becomes visible ahead, veer left through an open gate formed by large steel poles, and downhill. This section of the road is seldom maintained; watch for ruts.

1.6 Pedal right at a T intersection, toward I-15.

1.7 Drop left and ride through a drainage culvert under the freeway. Watch for large rocks in the tunnel, which can be hard to see in semi-darkness. The trail becomes sandy singletrack when it emerges from the tunnel, and the first few yards are rocky. Watch for petroglyphs on basalt rocks near the trail (look, but please don't touch or otherwise damage them).

1.9 Bear left (northwest) at a fork. Crank on up the slickrock, zigzagging toward the left side of the red cliff ahead. The trail is marked with occasional rock cairns and faded yellow paint. Side trails confuse the route, so follow these directions carefully.

2.3 Ride northeast along fun slickrock ledges, paralleling the top of the cliff. Note the water tank, still visible on the far side of the freeway. Use it as a reference during the ride to gauge your progress. Speaking of the view, you can see the white cliffs and towers of Zion National Park ahead, and the 10,000-foot Pine Valley Mountains loom above to your left.

3.2 Drop right down a short, steep descent; the trail doubles back below the cliff you've been following and heads southwest.

3.6 Go left to ride a short but fun little slickrock hogback.

3.8 Stay right at this intersection (you should be riding generally parallel to the base of the red cliff).

4.1 Zoom down a sandstone slab to a drainage, then up to the left without crossing it.

4.2 Now hang a sharp right, then left, into the bottom of the same drainage.

4.3 Merge with an old road that comes in from the left.

4.4 Junction with the start of the loop; go left, toward the freeway, and ride through the culvert and back the way you came.

5.1 Stay right at the junction with the road to the water tank.

6.4 Telegraph Street and the trailhead.

Warner Valley

Location: About 11 miles east of St. George.

Distance: 17.4 miles out and back.

Time: 4 hours.

Tread: 17.4 miles on maintained dirt.

Aerobic level: Moderate.

Technical difficulty: 1+.

Hazards: A few sandy spots, ruts, and occasional rocks. Heat and dehydration are major hazards during the summer; this ride is recommended for fall, winter, and spring. After a rain, allow a couple of days for the road to dry.

Highlights: An easy cruise through a very scenic valley. Points of interest include the ruins of a pioneer fort and very well preserved dinosaur tracks. It is suitable for families and beginners if you drive beyond the normal starting point to shorten the ride.

Land status: Bureau of Land Management; state of Utah; private.

Maps: USGS Washington Dome, The Divide.

Access: From St. George, drive northeast on Interstate 15 and exit at Washington. Turn right onto Green Springs Drive, then left on Telegraph Street. Next, turn right on 300 East and go south 3.7 miles, then turn left at a sign for Warner Valley. Turn left again 6 miles from Telegraph Street, onto the Warner Valley Road. Continue 1.1 miles on this maintained dirt road and park at the top of the hill, across from a large water tank. If desired, you can shorten the ride by continuing on the Warner Valley Road as far as you like.

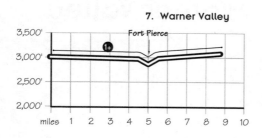

7. Warner Valley

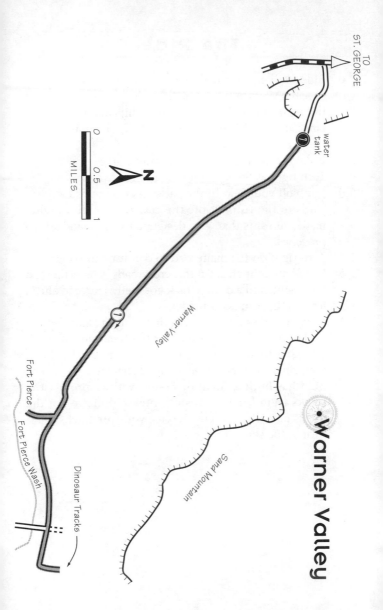

TO
ST. GEORGE

water
tank

1

Warner Valley

Sand Mountain

1

Fort Pierce

Fort Pierce Wash

Dinosaur Tracks

N

MILES

0   0.5   1

•Warner Valley

The Ride

0.0 Ride southeast through the broad valley. The red cliffs of Sand Mountain border the valley to the north, and the escarpment of the Hurricane Cliffs loom in the distance ahead. The road is essentially level, but it features a few gentle climbs and descents.

2.9 Pedal through a small area of sand dunes.

4.5 Turn right at the sign for Fort Pierce.

5.0 Jump off your bike at the parking area and walk a few yards to the ruins. Note the classic, though roughly made, gun slits that were designed to command all approaches.

5.5 Turn right on the main road to continue the ride.

7.5 Cruise straight ahead at this crossroads. The main road goes right, and a doubletrack goes left. The road ahead leads to the dinosaur tracks.

8.1 Rumble across a cattleguard then hang a sharp left.

8.7 End of the ride at the dinosaur track parking area. It's 300 yards to the tracks along a wide foot trail. The fossil footprints are exposed on a slab of shale in a wash. The BLM has built a small diversion wall to protect the tracks from further erosion; please don't touch the tracks or walk on them. Retrace your tire tracks to return to the start of the ride.

Dutchman Trail

Location: About 10 miles southeast of St. George.

Distance: 7.9-mile loop.

Time: 1.5 hours.

Tread: 7.9 miles on doubletrack.

Aerobic level: Easy.

Technical difficulty: 2.

Hazards: Occasional ruts and deep sand or gravel. There are a few rocky sections. Most of the trail turns to sticky mud during a rain; wait a day or two for it to dry out before riding it.

Highlights: An easy loop ride through an open valley, with an option to visit a petroglyph site. This ride is suitable for beginners; it has little technical difficulty or elevation gain.

Land status: Bureau of Land Management.

Maps: USGS Yellowhorse Flat.

Access: From St. George, drive northeast on Interstate 15 and exit at Washington. Turn right onto Green Springs Drive, then left on Telegraph Street. Next, turn right on 300 East and go south 3.7 miles, then turn left at a sign for Warner Valley. At 6.4 miles, the road changes to maintained dirt. Turn left at 9.2 miles, then right at 10 miles, crossing a cattleguard and a wash to reach the signed trailhead at 10.2 miles.

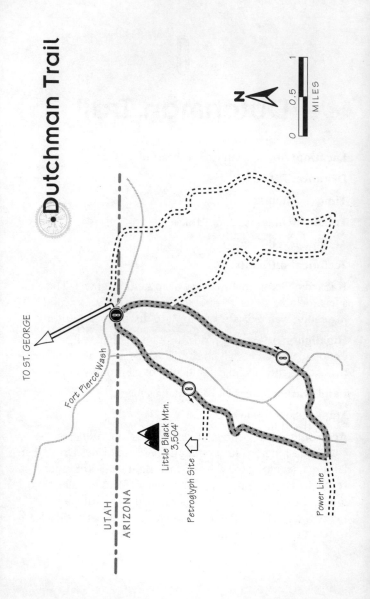

•Dutchman Trail

TO ST. GEORGE

Fort Pierce Wash

UTAH
ARIZONA

Little Black Mtn.
3,504'

Petroglyph Site

Power Line

8

8

8

N

0   0.5   1
MILES

8. Dutchman Trail

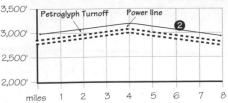

The Ride

0.0   There are two trails that start at this trailhead; to start on the Dutchman Trail, ride west along the fence.

0.1   Pedal left at the sign for Little Black Mountain. This section of the trail is smooth doubletrack, and it climbs very gradually up a broad valley.

1.9   Ride left at a bike trail marker pointing both ways. Take the right branch to explore a petroglyph site, which will add 0.6 mile of riding and about 0.5 mile of hiking to the trip.

3.7   Bear left at a minor fork just before a powerline.

3.9   Hang a sharp left at the powerline, and follow the road under the wires until the towers march up a steep hillside, then stay with the main road as it skirts the foot of the slope.

4.5   Stay left, on the main road.

5.3   Ride down and across a gravelly wash; the road may be vague for a few dozen yards.

6.1   A minor road merges from the right.

7.4   A major road joins from the right.

7.9   Trailhead.

Silver Reef

Location: About 16 miles northeast of St. George.

Distance: 25 miles one way. A car shuttle is required.

Time: 5 hours.

Tread: 21.8 miles on maintained dirt road; 3.2 miles on paved road.

Aerobic level: Strenuous.

Technical difficulty: 2+ on infrequently maintained dirt roads; 1 on paved roads.

Hazards: The road may have deep ruts, especially after wet weather. The last half is moderately rocky. Avoid this ride for a couple of days after rain, because it will be deep, sticky, ugly mud.

Highlights: Scenic cruise along the foothills of the Pine Valley Mountains.

Land status: Bureau of Land Management; Dixie National Forest; private; state of Utah.

Maps: USGS St. George, Washington, Harrisburg Junction, Signal Peak, Pintura; Dixie National Forest (Pine Valley and Cedar City ranger districts).

Access: First, set up a vehicle shuttle. From St. George, at the intersection of St. George Boulevard and Interstate 15, go west 0.2 mile, then turn right on 1000 East. Drive 0.2 mile to Skyline Drive, then turn right. Turn left on Industrial Road and

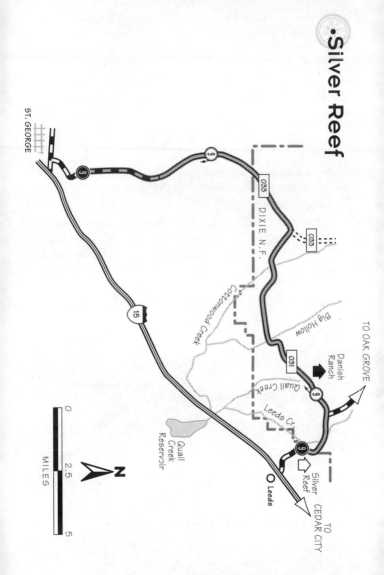

Silver Reef

ST. GEORGE

9

9

033

DIXIE N.F.

033

Cottonwood Creek

Big Hollow

031

9

TO OAK GROVE

Danish Ranch

Quail Creek

Leeds Cr.

9

Silver Reef

TO CEDAR CITY

Leeds

Quail Creek Reservoir

15

N

MILES

0   2.5   5

43

continue 0.4 mile. Turn left on Red Rock Road; leave a vehicle here for the end of the ride.

To reach the start of the ride from St. George, go north on I-15 about 14 miles to Leeds. After leaving the freeway, drive through the small settlement, then turn left and go under the freeway onto Forest Road 031. Continue 1.6 miles to the Dixie National Forest boundary and the end of the pavement.

The Ride

0.0 Start a steady climb on this smooth dirt road.

1.6 The route goes left, uphill, at the intersection with Oak Grove Road.

2.3 Coast down a hill to the Danish Ranch, then climb out the other side. The road continues in this fashion, descending to cross canyons and climbing the far side, for the first half of the ride.

6.9 Cross Big Hollow, a spectacular canyon.

9.2 Pedal over the top of a ridge and start the roll down into

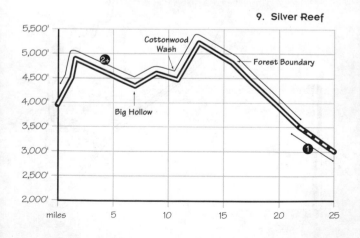

Cottonwood Canyon, the second major canyon along the route.

10.8 Crank up the climb out of Cottonwood Canyon.

12.9 Ride over the high point of the ride and start the long descent to St. George.

14.5 Note the change in the terrain—from soft sedimentary rocks to black lava flows. This causes a change in the road surface, from just plain rutted to rocky and rutted.

16.0 Coast out of the Dixie National Forest. The pinyon-juniper forest gives way to open sagebrush.

17.5 Start down a steeper section.

20.1 A road merges from the left.

21.8 Roll onto pavement, though with the potholes it may not be much smoother than the dirt.

25.0 The end of the ride at the intersection of Red Rock Road and Industrial Road.

Oak Grove

Location: About 16 miles northeast of St. George.

Distance: 15 miles out and back, or 7.5 miles all downhill with a car shuttle.

Time: 3 hours.

Tread: 7.5 miles on maintained dirt road.

Aerobic level: Strenuous.

Technical difficulty: 2.

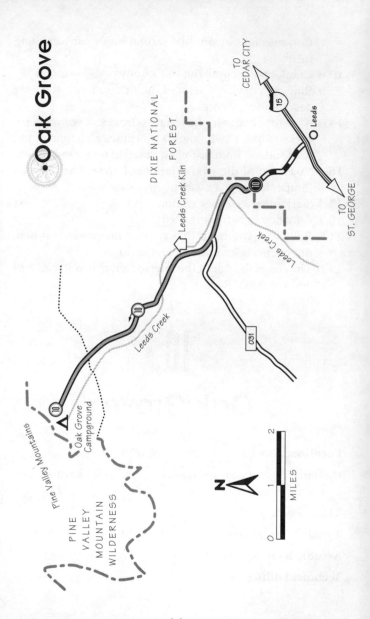

Oak Grove

TO CEDAR CITY

15

Leeds

TO ST. GEORGE

DIXIE NATIONAL FOREST

Leeds Creek Kiln

Leeds Creek

Leeds Creek

O51

Pine Valley Mountains

Oak Grove Campground

PINE VALLEY MOUNTAIN WILDERNESS

N

MILES

0   1   2

Hazards: Expect the usual early season ruts and a few rocky sections on the upper part of the road. Avoid this ride for a couple of days after rain to allow the mud to dry.

Highlights: Ride along Leeds Creek to the foot of the Pine Valley Mountains. There's also a historic charcoal kiln site you can check out.

Land status: Dixie National Forest.

Maps: USGS Pintura, Signal Peak; Dixie National Forest (Pine Valley and Cedar City ranger districts).

Access: From St. George, drive north on Interstate 15 to Leeds. After leaving the freeway, drive through the small settlement, then turn left and go under the freeway onto Forest Road 031. Continue 1.6 miles to the Dixie National Forest boundary and the end of the pavement.

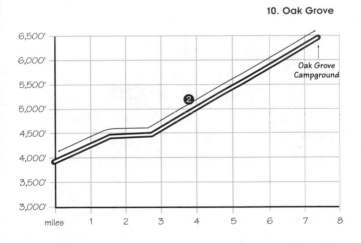

10. Oak Grove

0.0 Start a steady climb on this smooth dirt road.

1.6 FR 031 goes left. Our route goes right and downhill into the Leeds Creek drainage at this intersection.

2.7 An unmarked pullout signals the start of the short trail to the Leeds Creek Kiln. The well-preserved kiln was built in 1890 to make charcoal for silver refining at the Silver Reef Mine.

5.8 Pedal past the Three Pine Creek Trail on the left. The escarpment of the Pine Valley Mountains starts to take on impressive proportions.

7.5 Oak Grove Campground and the turn around point. Enjoy the downhill screamer back to the start—but watch for traffic!

J.E.M. Trail

Location: About 8 miles east of Hurricane.

Distance: 12.7-mile loop.

Time: 2 to 3 hours.

Tread: 6.1 miles on singletrack; 4.4 miles on doubletrack; 2.2 miles on maintained dirt road.

Aerobic level: Moderate.

Technical difficulty: 3 on singletrack; 2 on doubletrack; 1 on maintained dirt.

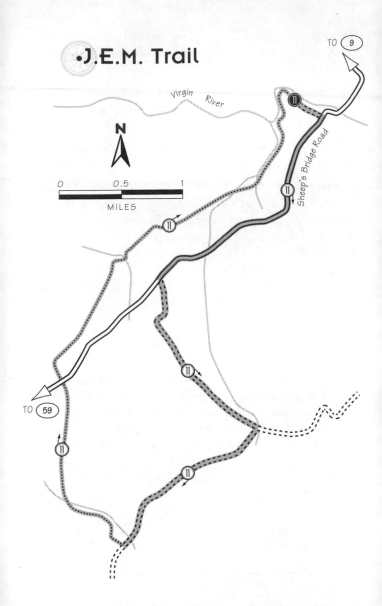

•J.E.M. Trail

Virgin River

TO ⑨

⑪

Sheep's Bridge Road

⑪

N

0   0.5   1

MILES

⑪

⑪

TO ㊼

⑪

⑪

Hazards: Some dropoffs toward the end of the ride. This is not a good choice right after a rain—allow a couple of days for the tread to dry.

Highlights: A long, fun singletrack descent with a scenic canyon rim ride as a treat at the end. This fine trail was named for the initials of John, Ellen, and Mike, who developed it.

Land status: Bureau of Land Management.

Maps: USGS Virgin, Hurricane.

Access: From St. George, drive north on Interstate 15 about 7 miles, then exit onto Utah Highway 9. Continue through Hurricane, past the junction with UT 59, toward Zion National Park on UT 9. At the Mile 17 marker (7.7 miles from the junction of UT 9 and UT 59), turn right onto Sheep's Bridge Road, an unmarked, maintained dirt road. Cross Sheep's Bridge, then turn right onto the first doubletrack and drive 0.2 mile to the end of the road, overlooking the Virgin River.

The Ride

- **0.0** Begin by pedaling back the way you drove in.
- **0.2** Hang a right onto Sheep's Bridge Road. You'll be climbing steadily as the road winds in and out of drainages.
- **2.4** Ride left onto an unsigned doubletrack, just past a minor wash. The road goes in and out of the wash as it

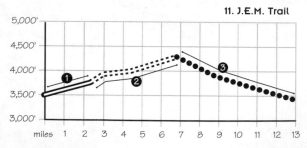

11. J.E.M. Trail

climbs toward the slopes of Gooseberry Mesa ahead. Don't be tempted to ride the wash—it's soft and sandy.

3.1 Go through a wire gate, and start to climb more steeply.

4.4 Turn right at this road intersection. The doubletrack climbs more gradually now as it winds around the terraced terrain at the foot of the mesa. As a reward for the climb, the view opens out to the west, with the Pine Valley Mountains dominating the skyline.

5.2 Pass through another wire gate.

6.6 Turn sharply right onto singletrack, which is marked by two rock cairns. (If you arrive at a gate, you've gone 300 yards too far.) This is the highest elevation along the ride. The narrow but mostly smooth singletrack winds through the sage and makes its way down the ridge to the northwest.

7.0 Go around the end of a fence, then drop into a small canyon.

7.5 Emerge from the end of the canyon and continue the descent.

8.3 Cross a maintained dirt road (the main road you started the ride on) and continue on singletrack west of the road.

8.7 Ride across a minor doubletrack.

9.1 Go around a stock tank on the left.

9.5 Stay to the right as the singletrack merges briefly with an old doubletrack.

10.0 Drop into a gully, then swing right, upstream, to climb out of the drainage.

11.0 Ride down into a small canyon, staying on the left side at first.

11.3 As the canyon deepens, cross to its right side, following a few rock cairns across the slickrock where a doubletrack comes in from the east. (Riders with a fear of heights might want to bail out on this doubletrack, which takes you to Sheep's Bridge Road.) No vertigo?

Continue on singletrack along the rim of the inner gorge. Use caution, because there are some serious dropoffs next to the trail. Soon the canyon ends at the Virgin River, and you'll ride upstream on the rim of the river canyon.

12.7 The trailhead and the end of the ride.

Gooseberry Mesa

Location: About 39 miles west of St. George.

Distance: 11.1-mile loop.

Time: 3 hours.

Tread: 10.2 miles on singletrack; 0.9 mile on doubletrack.

Aerobic level: Moderate.

Technical difficulty: 3 on singletrack; 4 with sections of 5+ on slickrock; 2 on doubletrack.

Hazards: Occasional sudden, sharp turns and low branches on singletrack; sharp drops and climbs on slickrock; and a few dropoffs near trail. The mesa is nearly flat and the trail has many twists and turns. To keep oriented, take note of two major landmarks before leaving the trailhead. Prominent, double-summited Smithsonian Butte lies directly east, and West Temple, a flat-topped white monolith with a red cap, lies northeast. If you lose the trail, bail out to the road, which is either north or south of you, depending on which rim you were riding. Then cruise east to the trailhead.

Highlights: About equally split between slickrock and smooth singletrack, this is a varied and challenging ride. Long sections of trail follow the 1,000-foot rim of Gooseberry Mesa, providing spectacular views of southwest Utah, including the Pine Valley Mountains and the temples of Zion National Park. The Left Fork Road continues west from the trailhead most of the way to The Point at the west end of the mesa and provides access to the trails at several points, so you can ride any portion of the loop and then use the road for a quick return to the trailhead. Intermediate riders can walk the technical sections. Numerous large slickrock patches provide opportunities for riders of all abilities. These range from almost parking lot–smooth to extreme technical challenges. There are many unimproved campsites along Gooseberry and Left Fork roads; please use "leave-no-trace" camping techniques, especially with regard to campfires and human sanitation.

Land status: Bureau of Land Management; private; state of Utah.

Map: USGS Virgin.

Access: The last 0.5 mile of the access road crosses private land; access to the trailhead will likely be changed in the near future. Check with the BLM or a bike shop in St. George or Springdale for the latest changes.

From Springdale, drive 4 miles west on Utah Highway 9 to the east end of Rockville, then turn left (south) on Bridge Road. Go 1.6 miles, crossing the Virgin River bridge, then turn left at a T intersection onto Smithsonian Butte Scenic Backway. Continue on this maintained dirt road 4.9 miles, then turn right (west) on signed Gooseberry Mesa Road, also maintained dirt. After 3.6 miles, turn left on an unsigned doubletrack (Left Fork Road) and go 1 mile to the trailhead at a cattleguard. This road is suitable for normal vehicles if driven with care.

From St. George, drive north about 7 miles on Interstate 15, then go east on UT 9 at the Hurricane exit. In Hurricane,

Gooseberry Mesa

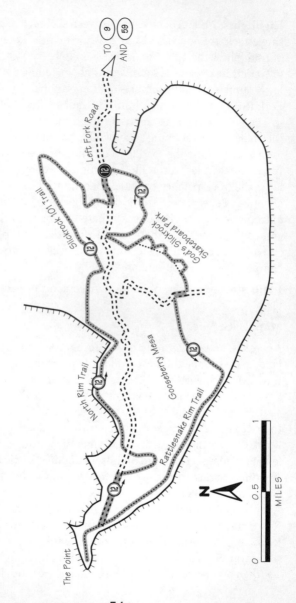

turn right on UT 59, drive west 14.4 miles, then turn left (north) onto Smithsonian Butte Scenic Backway, a maintained dirt road. This turnoff is unmarked and is between mile markers 9 and 8. Go north 2.9 miles, then turn left at Gooseberry Mesa Road. Drive another 3.6 miles, then turn left on the Left Fork Road and go 1 mile to the trailhead.

The Ride

0.0 Although this ride can be done in either direction, this description follows it clockwise, the most popular way. Start on the singletrack just west of the cattleguard on the south side of the parking area and cruise through pinyon-juniper woodland.

0.6 Follow green paint dots and rock cairns across slickrock as the trail turns right to skirt a small canyon.

1.1 The singletrack touches Left Fork Road at the head of the canyon, then veers south along its west rim into God's Slickrock Skateboard Park.

1.8 The trail splits; go left, which is the more technical variation. The right fork is easier. There are two more splits in the next half mile; stay left at each. These small loops were the first slickrock rides pioneered on Gooseberry. Some of this section is marked in white paint.

2.5 Hang a right on doubletrack.

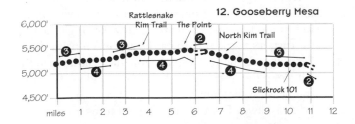

12. Gooseberry Mesa

2.6 Pedal left on singletrack to start the Rattlesnake Rim Trail (the doubletrack goes north about 0.5 mile to Left Fork Road).

3.6 Ride up to the south rim of the mesa and another incredible southern Utah view. When you're done gawking, follow the singletrack and slickrock trail west along the rim.

5.1 Turn left onto Left Fork Road; in a few yards, follow singletrack left, then west. This section is marked with yellow paint dots.

5.5 Pedal out onto The Point, the western tip of Gooseberry Mesa. The rock narrows to a few feet at the end and the dropoffs are serious. The awesome view extends from the 10,000-foot Pine Valley Mountains to the west, to the white temples of Zion National Park to the northeast. Directly below, to the northwest, you're looking at the J.E.M. Trail (see Ride 11). After you've had enough, retrace your route back to the main loop.

5.9 Left Fork Road; go left on this rough doubletrack to continue the loop.

6.5 Hang a right at a cairn to start on Sand Pit Bypass Trail, which avoids a nasty stretch of sand on the doubletrack. Loop south, then back north, following yellow paint dots across slickrock.

7.0 Go right on Left Fork Road, then almost immediately left on singletrack at a cairn to start the Dam Trail. (From here, Left Fork Road will take you back to the trailhead in 2.4 miles of fast, easy cruising, if you want.)

7.1 Ride up to the north rim and follow the singletrack to the east; it's marked with cairns and green paint dots.

8.2 Pedal over the dam at a stock tank, then continue to the left along the north rim. (Left Fork Road is 100 yards southeast of the dam.)

8.4 Veer east away from the rim, which turns north.

9.0 Turn left at a junction to start the Slickrock 101 Trail. (The right fork goes about 100 yards to Left Fork Road, meeting it at a sharp S turn 0.8 mile from the trailhead.) Ride singletrack and slickrock east for about a mile, then turn sharply right as the trail heads southwest. Cairns and green dots mark the trail, but it gets a little vague after it crosses a doubletrack. If you lose it, go south (or follow the doubletrack) to Left Fork Road.

10.8 Go left on Left Fork Road and cruise 0.3 mile east to the trailhead at the cattleguard.

11.1 Trailhead.

Left Fork Road Option: For an easy family ride, cruise Left Fork Road to The Point, 6 miles out and back.

Gooseberry Mesa Road Option: Ride Left Fork Road, Gooseberry Mesa Road, Smithsonian Butte Scenic Backway, and UT 9 back to Springdale. It's a fast, mostly downhill cruise, but you'll have to arrange for someone to pick you up in Springdale.

Grafton

Location: About 4 miles west of Springdale.

Distance: 7 miles out and back.

Time: 2 hours.

Tread: 1.8 miles paved; 5.2 miles maintained dirt road.

Aerobic level: Easy.

Technical difficulty: 1 on maintained dirt and paved roads.

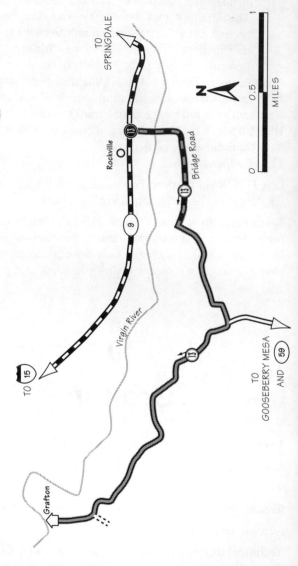

Grafton

TO SPRINGDALE

N

MILES
0   0.5   1

Rockville

9

13

13

Bridge Road

13

Virgin River

TO 15

TO GOOSEBERRY MESA AND 59

Grafton

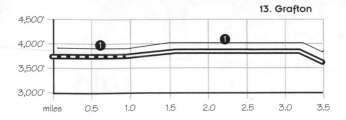

Hazards: Tourist traffic on road.

Highlights: Scenic, easy ride to an abandoned, historic settlement used as the movie set for *Butch Cassidy and the Sundance Kid*. The old buildings and a pioneer cemetery are interesting to explore.

Land status: Bureau of Land Management; private.

Map: USGS Springdale West.

Access: From Springdale, drive about 4 miles west on Utah Highway 9 to Rockville. Park near the east end of town, at Bridge Road.

The Ride

0.0 Ride south on paved Bridge Road and cross the historic steel bridge across the Virgin River. The road turns right.

0.9 End of pavement. The maintained dirt road goes left up a moderate but short hill.

1.6 At a T intersection, turn right.

3.2 A short spur road goes left to the Grafton Cemetery.

3.5 The old town of Grafton. Feel free to explore but use caution. Watch for holes in floors and other hazards. Be careful not to touch or damage anything.

Springdale Start Option: Start the ride in Springdale, which adds 7 miles of pavement, out and back.

Red Mountain

Location: About 1 mile east of Cedar City.

Distance: 2.8-mile loop with a cherry stem (see Glossary).

Time: 1 hour.

Tread: 2.6 miles on singletrack; 0.2 mile on doubletrack.

Aerobic level: Moderate.

Technical difficulty: 3 and 4 on singletrack; 2 on doubletrack.

Hazards: Sudden sharp descents and dropoffs near trail. Watch for ATVs on the far end of the loop.

Highlights: Challenging singletrack that is easily accessible from town. A good ride during the cooler months when the high country is snow covered.

Land status: Private.

Map: USGS Cedar City.

Access: From the intersection of Business 15 and Utah Highway 14 (Main Street and Center Street) in Cedar City, drive east 0.9 mile on UT 14. Park on the left 100 yards before the truck turnaround/chainup area.

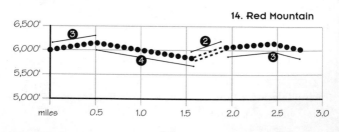

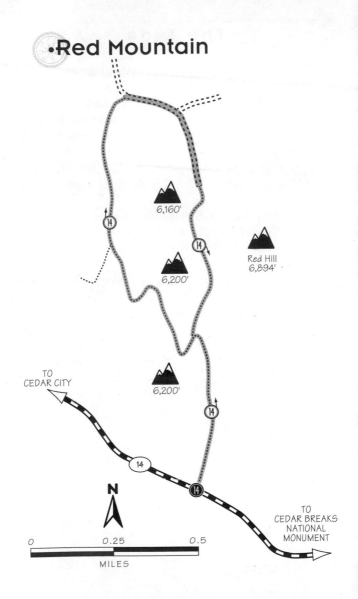

•Red Mountain

6,160'

14

14

Red Hill
6,894'

6,200'

TO
CEDAR CITY

6,200'

14

14

N

14

TO
CEDAR BREAKS
NATIONAL
MONUMENT

0   0.25   0.5

MILES

61

The Ride

0.0   Ride up the obvious singletrack that follows the wash to the north.

0.5   Hang a sharp left at the singletrack fork. The correct trail almost doubles back the way you came. Ride across a ridge, then traverse a slope to reach a razorback descent. Use caution; there are dropoffs on either side.

1.1   Stay to the right as you cross a small valley with several ATV tracks joining from the left. Head north toward a pass.

1.6   Turn right (east) and pedal up a dirt road above a golf course; then turn right (south) again onto a doubletrack that enters a canyon. The trail becomes singletrack as it climbs steeply.

1.9   At a pass, turn sharply right and descend into a gully, then climb toward the pass to the south.

2.3   Ride up onto the pass where you entered the loop; turn left to descend to the trailhead. Keep your speed under control and be alert for riders coming up the trail.

2.8   Back at the trailhead. You could do the whole thing again!

Blowhard Mountain

Location: About 13 miles east of Cedar City.

Distance: 11.7-mile loop.

Time: 3 hours.

Tread: 3 miles on singletrack; 0.8 mile on doubletrack; 1.1 miles on maintained dirt road, 6.8 miles on paved road.

Aerobic level: Strenuous.

Technical difficulty: 4 with sections of 5 on singletrack; 2 on doubletrack, 1 on maintained dirt and paved roads.

Hazards: Steep, loose, rocky trail, with dropoffs near the trail. Traffic on Utah Highway 14.

Highlights: A technical trail for expert riders, this trail skirts the edge of Ashdown Gorge Wilderness, with dramatic views of the eroded canyons of the Pink Cliffs. Intermediate riders can walk the technical sections.

Land status: Dixie National Forest.

Maps: USGS Navajo Lake, Webster Flat; Dixie National Forest (#702) Trails Illustrated; Dixie National Forest (Pine Valley and Cedar City ranger districts).

Access: From Cedar City, drive about 13 miles east on Utah Highway 14, then turn left (north) at the signed turnoff to Crystal Springs and park.

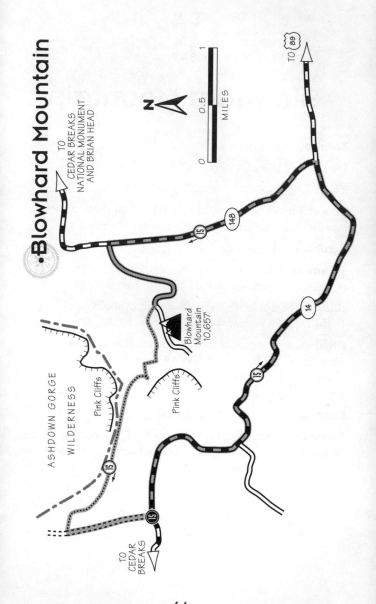

•Blowhard Mountain

TO
CEDAR BREAKS
NATIONAL MONUMENT
AND BRIAN HEAD

N

ASHDOWN GORGE
WILDERNESS

Pink Cliffs

Pink Cliffs

Blowhard Mountain
10,657

TO
CEDAR BREAKS

TO 89

0   0.5   1
MILES

14B

14

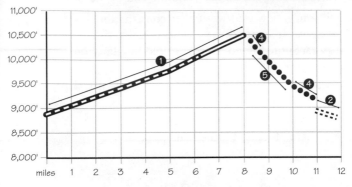

The Ride

0.0 Ride east on UT 14 as the paved highway climbs steadily onto the high plateau. This road is busy; be alert for tourists who are not watching the road.

4.7 Turn left (north) on UT 148 toward Cedar Breaks National Monument. The road continues a steady climb.

6.8 After the highway emerges into an expansive alpine meadow and the climb moderates, turn left onto the unsigned, maintained dirt road to Blowhard Mountain.

7.9 The signed trailhead for the Blowhard Mountain Trail; turn right (north) and follow the trail as it traverses around the north side of the mountain. It soon begins a steep descent in several switchbacks, then follows a powerline down several steep drops. Next, the trail descends an orange limestone ridge with a precipitous drop on the right side. Work your way down steep, loose, narrow switchbacks (some riders will want to walk). The trail becomes easy where it goes under the powerline again. Cruise on.

10.9 Turn left (south) on the Crystal Springs Road, an easy doubletrack. It climbs a few yards then descends.

11.7 UT 14, your vehicle, and the end of the ride.

Option: A new trail was under construction at the time this book was researched. It would continue farther west from the Crystal Springs Road. Check with local bike shops for the latest information.

Shuttle Option: Many locals prefer to do this ride one way with a car shuttle. To do this, leave a vehicle at the Crystal Springs turnoff, then follow the ride description above to the Blowhard Mountain turnoff and park.

Cedar Breaks

Location: About 18 miles east of Cedar City.

Distance: 17.6 miles out and back.

Time: 4 hours.

Tread: 17.6 miles on paved road.

Aerobic level: Moderate.

Technical difficulty: 1.

Hazards: Tourist traffic on the park road.

Highlights: A road ride in a mountain bike book? This road is so spectacular you just have to do it. Besides, one of the great things about a mountain bike is that it works pretty well on pavement too. Bikes are not allowed on trails in Cedar Breaks National Monument, so this is the only option for seeing this fine scenery on a bike.

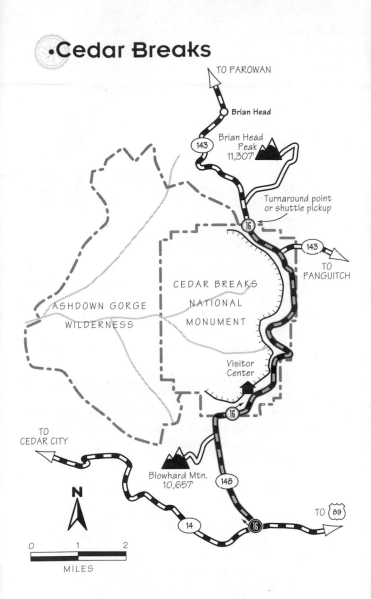

•Cedar Breaks

TO PAROWAN

Brian Head

Brian Head
Peak
11,307'

Turnaround point
or shuttle pickup

143

16

143

TO
PANGUITCH

CEDAR BREAKS
NATIONAL
MONUMENT

ASHDOWN GORGE
WILDERNESS

Visitor
Center

16

TO
CEDAR CITY

Blowhard Mtn.
10,657'

148

N

14

16

TO 89

0   1   2
MILES

Land status: Dixie National Forest; Cedar Breaks National Monument.

Maps: USGS Brian Head, Navajo Lake; Dixie National Forest (#702) Trails Illustrated; Cedar Breaks National Monument brochure.

Access: From Cedar City, drive about 18 miles east on Utah Highway 14, turn left on UT 148 toward Cedar Breaks, then park on the right. If you have two vehicles, you can do this ride one way. Leave a vehicle here and drive 8.8 miles on UT 148 and UT 143 to the north boundary of the national monument.

The Ride

0.0 Pedal up the unrelenting hill on UT 148. After about a mile, the highway emerges into a broad alpine meadow and the climb moderates.

3.6 The Visitor Center and Point Supreme. You've done the steepest climb of the ride. Stop here to enjoy the view and pick up a brochure, which explains the features of the park.

5.7 Chessman Overlook, which gives you a view of rock towers that look like giant chess pieces.

6.8 Alpine Pond. There's no view here from the road, but a foot (only) trail leads to Alpine Pond and back to Chessman Overlook. Bring a bike lock if you plan to hike this trail.

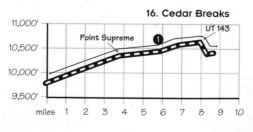

7.8 The junction with UT 143 and the high point of the ride. Continue straight ahead on UT 143, which descends gently.

8.3 North View, which offers a look back across Cedar Breaks to the Point Supreme area.

8.8 The national monument boundary and the turnaround. This point offers a sweeping view of Brian Head Peak and the Mammoth Creek Valley.

Navajo Lake Loop

Location: About 25 miles east of Cedar City.

Distance: 11.4-mile loop.

Time: 3 hours.

Tread: 10.4 miles on singletrack; 0.6 mile on doubletrack; 0.4 mile on maintained dirt road.

Aerobic level: Moderate.

Technical difficulty: 3 on singletrack; 2 on doubletrack; 1 on maintained dirt road.

Hazards: Some rocky sections.

Highlights: A very scenic loop around Navajo Lake that passes through a rugged lava flow. The ride is mostly level except for a climb and descent in the first 2.6 miles.

Land status: Dixie National Forest.

•Navajo Lake Loop

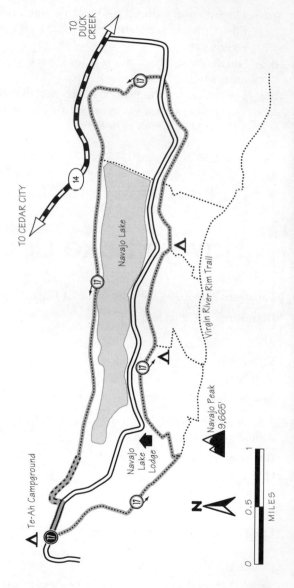

Maps: USGS Navajo Lake; Dixie National Forest (#702) Trails Illustrated; Dixie National Forest (Pine Valley and Cedar City ranger districts).

Access: From Cedar City, drive east on Utah Highway 14 about 25 miles, then turn right (south) on maintained dirt Navajo Lake Road. Continue to the end of the road and park at Virgin River Rim Trailhead just past Te-Ah Campground.

The Ride

0.0   Te-Ah Trailhead; ride south and east on Virgin River Rim Trail, which climbs steadily through the forest.

1.5   Turn left onto the Lodge Trail and roll down a series of switchbacks.

2.6   Pedal straight ahead on Navajo Lake Trail, paralleling the south shore of the lake.

3.5   At Navajo Lake Campground, Navajo Trail branches right; continue straight ahead (east) on the level Navajo Lake Trail.

4.5   Pass through Spruces Campground (Spruces Trail branches right).

5.4   Cross Dike Trail and continue east.

6.1   Cross Navajo Lake Road and pedal north on Navajo Lake Trail as it skirts the east end of the lake.

6.5   Ride into a spectacular lava area.

6.8   The lava ends and the trail turns west, passing through aspens.

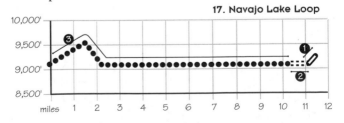

7.6 A short spur trail goes left to the dike that divides the lake.

10.4 Ride onto doubletrack at the west end of the lake.

10.8 Hang a right on Navajo Lake Road.

11.1 Pedal past Te-Ah Campground.

11.4 Trailhead at the Virgin River Rim Trail.

(Thanks to Kent Traveller of Cedar City Ranger District, Dixie National Forest, for providing this ride description.)

Cascade Falls Loop

Location: About 29 miles east of Cedar City.

Distance: 16.2-mile loop.

Time: 4 hours.

Tread: 11.9 miles on singletrack; 4.3 miles on maintained dirt road.

Aerobic level: Strenuous.

Technical difficulty: 3 on singletrack; 1 on roads.

Hazards: Short rocky sections on singletrack, traffic on roads.

Highlights: Spectacular, panoramic views of the Pink Cliffs and Zion National Park.

Land status: Dixie National Forest.

Maps: USGS Navajo Lake, Henrie Knolls, Straight Canyon, Strawberry Point; Dixie National Forest (#702) Trails Illustrated; Dixie National Forest (Pine Valley and Cedar City ranger districts).

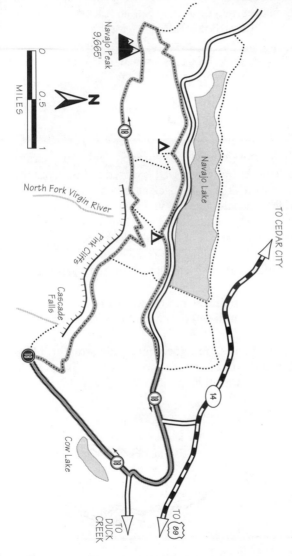

Cascade Falls Loop

Navajo Peak
9,665

18

North Fork Virgin River

Pink Cliffs

Cascade Falls

Navajo Lake

18

18

TO CEDAR CITY

18

Cow Lake

18

14

TO DUCK CREEK

TO 89

N

MILES

0   0.5   1

Access: From Cedar City, drive east on Utah Highway 14 about 25 miles, then turn right (south) on Navajo Lake Road, a maintained dirt road. After 0.3 mile, turn left (east) on another maintained dirt road, signed for Duck Creek and Cascade Falls. Turn right (southwest) after 1.1 miles onto signed Cascade Falls Road, and continue 1.6 miles to the end of the road.

The Ride

0.0 Before starting the ride, be sure to check out Cascade Falls. This 0.5-mile spur trail is closed to bikes, but the falls are worth the walk. Back at the parking area, start the ride by pedaling up the Virgin River Rim Trail to the northwest. The wide singletrack climbs onto the Virgin River Rim in a series of switchbacks.

0.9 Top of the steep climb. The trail skirts the edge of the Pink Cliffs, with views to Zion National Park and beyond.

1.5 An eroded amphitheater in the limestone Pink Cliffs rivals anything at the more famous Cedar Breaks or Bryce Canyon.

2.1 The signed Dike Trail goes right; ride straight. (This trail, and the next two, are spur trails to the Navajo Lake Road, and can be used to shorten the loop. Each is about 0.5 mile long.)

2.5 Start a short descent.

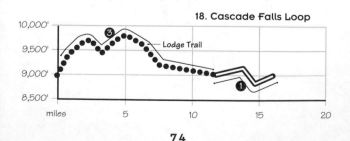

3.6 Junction with Spruces Trail in a saddle; go straight.

4.3 Navajo Trail goes right, but ride straight, continuing along the rim.

5.1 From the highest point on the ride, the trail starts to descend, skirting the north side of Navajo Peak.

6.4 Hang a right on the Lodge Trail, and descend several switchbacks.

7.4 Pedal straight ahead on Navajo Lake Trail, paralleling the south shore of the lake.

8.3 At Navajo Lake Campground, Navajo Trail branches right; continue straight ahead (east) on the level Navajo Lake Trail.

9.3 Pass through Spruces Campground (Spruces Trail branches right).

10.2 Cross Dike Trail and continue east.

11.9 Turn right onto Navajo Lake Road, a maintained dirt road.

13.5 Turn right (southeast) onto the signed Duck Creek-Cascade Falls Road, and cruise down the hill (watch for oncoming traffic).

14.6 Turn right (southwest) onto the signed Cascade Falls Road. This is an easy climb through Dry Valley.

16.2 Cascade Falls Trailhead and the end of the ride.

Virgin River Rim Trail Option: This loop ride uses part of the Virgin River Rim Trail. Some riders prefer to do the Virgin River Rim Trail one way with a car shuttle. To do this, leave a vehicle at Strawberry Point at the end of the ride. See Strawberry Point Loop (Ride 20) for trailhead directions, and Strawberry Point Loop and Ice Cave Loop (Ride 19) for ride directions.

(Thanks to Kent Traveller of Cedar City Ranger District, Dixie National Forest, for providing part of this ride description.)

Ice Cave Loop

Location: About 27 miles east of Cedar City.

Distance: 11.6-mile loop.

Time: 3 hours.

Tread: 3.5 miles on singletrack; 4.6 miles on doubletrack; 3.5 miles on maintained dirt road.

Aerobic level: Strenuous.

Technical difficulty: 3 with sections of 3+ on singletrack; 2 on doubletrack; 1 on maintained dirt road.

Hazards: The trail skirts the edge of cliffs in a few places.

Highlights: The singletrack runs along the edge of the Virgin River Rim and provides excellent views of the Pink Cliffs.

Land status: Dixie National Forest.

Maps: USGS Strawberry Point; Dixie National Forest Trails (#702) Illustrated; Dixie National Forest (Pine Valley and Cedar City ranger districts).

Access: From Cedar City, drive about 27 miles east on Utah Highway 14 and park at the signed turnoff for Duck Creek Campground.

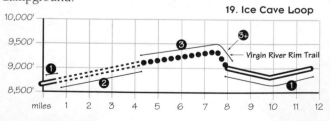

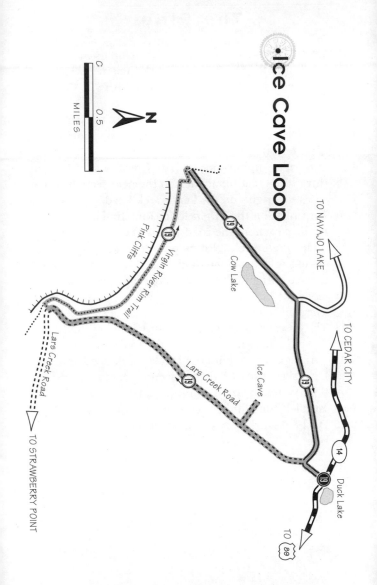

Ice Cave Loop

TO NAVAJO LAKE

TO CEDAR CITY

TO STRAWBERRY POINT

TO 89

Lars Creek Road

Lars Creek Road

Virgin River Rim Trail

Pink Cliffs

Cow Lake

Ice Cave

Duck Lake

MILES

N

The Ride

0.0   Cross the highway and ride the maintained dirt road south past the Duck Creek Work Center.

0.3   Turn left (southeast) and pedal (grunt!) up the steep road to Lars Creek.

1.0   Turn right (west) on the signed road to the Ice Cave.

1.3   The road ends at the Ice Cave. After checking out the cave, return to the Lars Creek Road.

1.6   Turn right (uphill) on the Lars Creek Road. There are three roads that branch left in the next section—in all cases stay right, on the Lars Creek Road.

4.6   Turn right on the Virgin River Rim Trail at the signed trailhead where the road meets the rim. The trail, a wide singletrack, climbs parallel to the road. After about a mile the climb moderates. Watch for an amphitheater in the Pink Cliffs; it is probably the finest one along the Virgin River Rim Trail.

7.5   The trail starts to descend in a series of switchbacks.

8.1   The Cascade Falls Trailhead. Turn right here and cruise down the maintained dirt road into Dry Valley.

9.8   Turn right (east) onto the Duck Creek Road and cross Dry Valley. The road then descends next to a jagged lava flow. Watch for traffic on the road.

11.3   Turn left (downhill) and coast to the highway.

11.6   UT 14 at Duck Creek Campground and the end of the ride.

Strawberry Point Loop

Location: About 34 miles east of Cedar City.

Distance: 14.5-mile loop.

Time: 4 hours.

Tread: 5.9 miles on singletrack; 3.2 miles on doubletrack; 5.4 miles on maintained dirt road.

Aerobic level: Strenuous.

Technical difficulty: 3 with sections of 3+ on singletrack; 2 on doubletrack; 1 on maintained dirt road.

Hazards: The trail skirts the edge of cliffs in a few places.

Highlights: Excellent views from the Virgin River Rim; challenging singletrack.

Land status: Dixie National Forest; private.

Maps: USGS Strawberry Point; Dixie National Forest Trails (#702) Illustrated; Dixie National Forest (Pine Valley and Cedar City ranger districts).

Access: From Cedar City, drive about 30 miles east on Utah

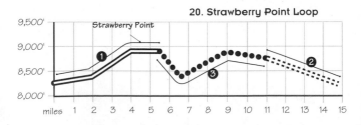

79

•Strawberry Point Loop

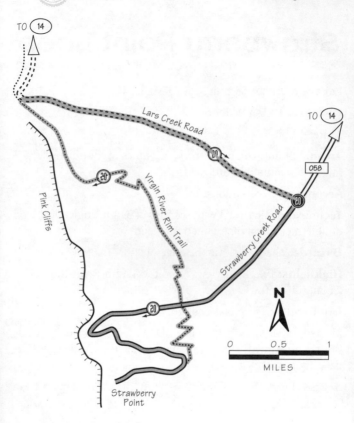

Highway 14, then turn right (south) at the signed Strawberry Creek Road, which is maintained dirt. Continue 4 miles, then park at the signed junction with the Lars Creek Road (Forest Road 059), which forks to the right (west).

The Ride

0.0 Start by pedaling up Strawberry Creek Road.

1.8 Cross Virgin River Rim Trail and continue on Strawberry Creek Road, which passes through a subdivision. Continue straight; don't take any turns.

4.2 Virgin River Rim Trailhead; ignore it for now and continue to the end of the road.

4.8 The end of the road at Strawberry Point. Hide your bike, or walk it to Strawberry Point. After enjoying the panorama, ride back down the road to Virgin River Rim Trailhead.

5.4 Turn right (east) onto Virgin River Rim Trail. The wide singletrack swoops down the densely forested hillside in a series of switchbacks; definitely more challenging than the road up!

6.6 Cross Strawberry Creek Road. The singletrack starts to switchback up a climb. Occasionally it joins a short section of doubletrack. The trail crosses a drainage and climbs more switchbacks to finally reach the Virgin River Rim.

9.0 The trail follows the rim westward, staying level or descending slightly.

10.4 Another spectacular eroded amphitheater. The standing rock towers are called hoodoos; this area has a number of fine examples.

11.3 Virgin River Rim Trail meets a doubletrack road; turn right (east) and descend along Lars Creek Road.

14.5 Strawberry Creek Road and the end of the ride.

Yankee Meadows

Location: About 8 miles north of Brian Head.

Distance: 16-mile loop.

Time: 3 hours.

Tread: 14.4 miles on maintained dirt road/doubletrack; 1.6 miles on paved road.

Aerobic level: Strenuous.

Technical difficulty: 2+ on dirt roads; 1 on paved roads.

Hazards: Tourist traffic on Utah Highway 143; watch your speed and look for oncoming traffic on steep descents.

Highlights: This is a good early summer ride, when the high country is still snowbound. The ride takes you past Vermillion Castle, Grand Castle, and other towering rock formations;

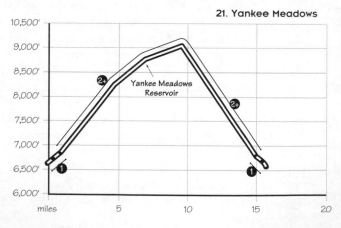

•Yankee Meadows

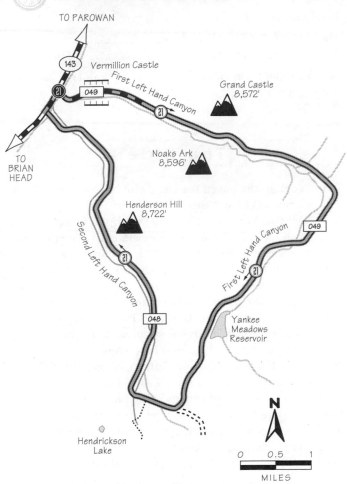

TO PAROWAN

143
21
049   Vermillion Castle
First Left Hand Canyon
21   Grand Castle
                     8,572'

TO
BRIAN
HEAD

                Noaks Ark
                8,596'

        Henderson Hill
        8,722'

Second Left Hand Canyon
                                    049
21   First Left Hand Canyon
                        21

048
                        Yankee
                        Meadows
                        Reservoir

N

0   0.5   1

Hendrickson
Lake   MILES

through two scenic canyons; and past a reservoir in an alpine setting.

Land status: Dixie National Forest; private.

Maps: USGS Parowan, Brian Head, Red Creek Reservoir; Dixie National Forest (Pine Valley and Cedar City ranger districts).

Access: From Brian Head, drive north on Utah Highway 143 about 8 miles, and park at the Yankee Meadows Road, Forest Road 049, which is a paved road going right (east).

The Ride

0.0 Pedal up the paved road as it climbs east through the Vermillion Castle area.

1.3 Ride past Vermilion Castle Campground (closed after a washout in 1997) as the pavement ends. The dirt road steepens as it climbs First Left Hand Canyon. Riders not into sustained climbs can turn back at any point. The reward for the climb is a series of alpine meadows along upper Bowery Creek, where the climb moderates.

4.6 Stay right at the junction with FR 359, the Robinson Reservoir Road. FR 049 now curves to the south.

7.1 Ride past Yankee Meadows Reservoir.

9.3 Whew! Top of the climb. Turn right onto FR 048 and start a steep descent into Second Left Hand Canyon. Keep your speed down and watch for uphill traffic.

9.8 The Dark Hollow Trail merges from the left.

15.2 Splash across the creek at an unbridged crossing.

15.7 Hang a right on UT 143.

16.0 Yankee Meadows Road and the trailhead.

(Thanks to Bill Murphy of Brian Head Cross Country Ski and Bike for providing the mileage log.)

Twisted Forest

Location: 2 miles west of Brian Head.

Distance: 10.2 miles out and back, plus an optional 1.2-mile hike.

Time: 3 hours.

Tread: 2.4 miles on doubletrack; 7.4 miles on maintained dirt roads.

Aerobic level: Moderate.

Technical difficulty: 1 on maintained dirt road; 2 on doubletrack.

Hazards: Road traffic; don't be caught on High Mountain during an afternoon thunderstorm.

Highlights: Panoramic views of Cedar Breaks National Monument, the Twisted Forest, and Brian Head Peak. Side hike to Twisted Forest (bring a bike lock).

Land status: Private; Dixie National Forest.

Maps: USGS Brian Head, Flanigan Arch.

Access: From the turnoff to the mall in the center of Brian Head, go 1.1 miles north on Utah Highway 143, then turn left

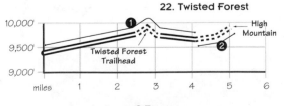

Twisted Forest

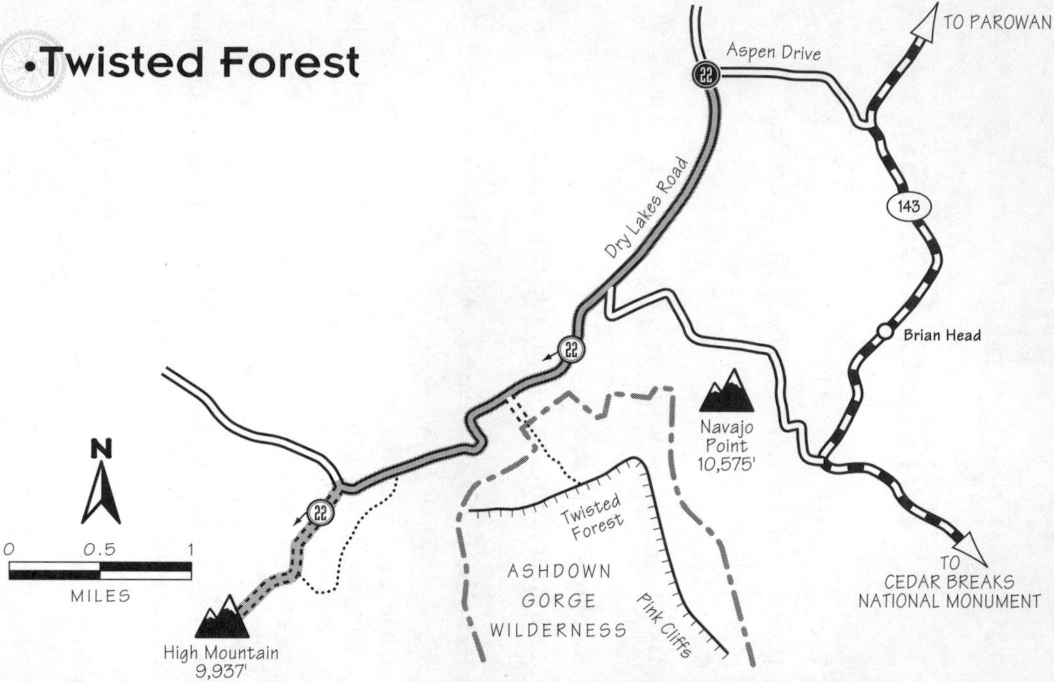

TO PAROWAN

143

Brian Head

TO CEDAR BREAKS NATIONAL MONUMENT

Aspen Drive

22

Dry Lakes Road

Navajo Point
10,575'

ASHDOWN GORGE WILDERNESS

Twisted Forest

Pink Cliffs

22

22

High Mountain
9,937'

N

0   0.5   1
MILES

(west) on Aspen Drive. Stay on the main road through the sub-division, over a pass, then down to the unsigned junction with the Dry Lakes Road at 1.3 miles. Park on the side of the road.

The Ride

0.0   Go left (south) on the maintained dirt Dry Lakes Road. The meadow soon gives way to shady aspens.

2.5   Turn left on the unsigned doubletrack to Twisted Forest Trailhead.

2.7   Twisted Forest Trailhead. Stash your bike and hike about 0.6 mile to the overlook. The trail lies in the Ashdown Gorge Wilderness and bikes are not allowed. But everyone should do the hike—the view is incredible. After the hike, pedal back out to the Dry Lakes Road.

2.9   Turn left on the Dry Lakes Road.

4.1   Turn left (south) on the signed High Mountain Road, and climb gradually through aspen stands on easy doubletrack.

4.7   Enter High Mountain Meadow. Turn right at the junction; the left fork can be taken on the return for an advanced singletrack descent (this option adds no distance).

5.1   Summit of High Mountain at 9,937 feet. The view includes Brian Head Peak, Ashdown Gorge, Cedar Breaks, Cedar City, and the desert ranges to the west. On clear days you can see 13,000-foot Wheeler Peak in Nevada, more than 100 miles to the northwest. To return, ride back the way you came.

Brian Head Start Option: You can start from UT 143 and ride Aspen Drive, which would add 2.6 miles to the total round-trip distance.

Pioneer Cabins

Location: In Brian Head.

Distance: 4.3-mile loop.

Time: 1 hour.

Tread: 0.3 mile paved; 0.8 mile on dirt roads; 3.2 miles on doubletrack with short sections of singletrack.

Aerobic level: Easy, with a few moderate sections.

Technical difficulty: 1 on roads; 2 on doubletrack and singletrack.

Hazards: Early season snowdrifts along the climb out of Pioneer Cabin Meadow.

Highlights: This is a good beginner ride. You'll ride through deep forest and alpine meadows on a loop past the ruins of historic log cabins.

Land status: Private; Dixie National Forest.

Maps: USGS Brian Head.

Access: From the turnoff to the mall in the center of Brian Head, go 0.7 mile north on Utah Highway 143, then turn right (east) and park at the start of the wide, dirt Burts Road.

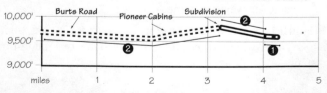

23. Pioneer Cabins

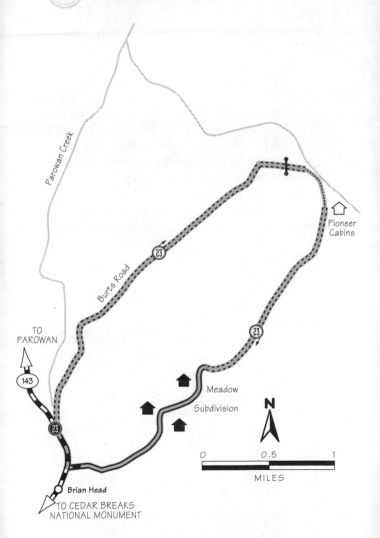

•Pioneer Cabins

Parowan Creek

Burts Road

㉓

㉓

Pioneer
Cabins

TO
PAROWAN

143

㉓

Meadow

Subdivision

N

TO CEDAR BREAKS
NATIONAL MONUMENT

Brian Head

0	0.5	1

MILES

The Ride

0.0   Pedal north on Burts Road. You'll descend a couple of gentle hills. Ignore the Town Trail, which soon cuts left and leaves the road.

1.7   Go through a gate at the end of Burts Road and descend on doubletrack. The hill steepens right at the end.

1.9   Cross a small creek, then turn right (south) on smooth singletrack and climb gradually into a meadow.

2.1   At an unsigned junction, turn left on singletrack, climb the short hill, then turn right on faint singletrack and ride (or walk) to the Pioneer Cabin ruins. After enjoying the cabins, return to the unsigned junction and continue straight ahead across the meadow.

2.2   The trail enters the forest and becomes doubletrack, which climbs steeply for a short distance, then passes several small lakes.

2.9   Cross a flat, pleasant meadow.

3.2   Enter a subdivision with confusing roads; bear generally left and downhill, aiming for the main road.

4.0   Roll onto pavement.

4.1   Turn right on UT 143.

4.3   Trailhead at the start of Burts Road on the right.

24

Scout Camp Loop

Location: In Brian Head.

Distance: 7.9-mile loop.

Time: 2 hours.

Tread: 6.2 miles on singletrack; 1.7 miles on doubletrack.

Aerobic level: Moderate.

Technical difficulty: 2 with sections of 3 on singletrack; 2 on doubletrack.

Hazards: Watch your speed on the downhills; there are sudden rocky sections. The first 2 miles of trail have seen recent logging activity; check with local bike shops for the latest information.

Highlights: Historic steam engine, and beautiful alpine meadows.

Land status: Dixie National Forest; private.

Maps: USGS Brian Head.

Access: From the turnoff to the mall in the center of Brian Head, drive 0.6 mile north on Utah Highway 143, then turn right (east) on the paved Bear Flat Road. After the road turns to dirt, continue up the steep subdivision road to a fork about 0.5 mile from the highway. Park along the side of the road just below the fork. Parking is limited; as an alternative, park at Burts Road, 0.1 mile north of the Bear Flat Road, and ride from there. This adds 1.2 miles to the ride.

•Scout Camp Loop

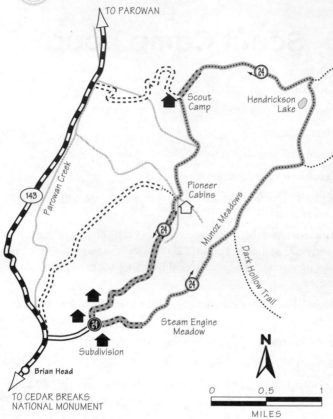

TO PAROWAN

Scout Camp

Hendrickson Lake

(24)

Parowan Creek

(143)

Pioneer Cabins

(24)

Munoz Meadows

Dark Hollow Trail

(24)

Steam Engine Meadow

Subdivision

(24)

Brian Head

TO CEDAR BREAKS
NATIONAL MONUMENT

N

0   0.5   1

MILES

The Ride

0.0   Go right at the fork and climb the hill to Steam Engine Meadow.

0.4   Go left on a doubletrack at a fork. Follow the left side of the meadow. The steam engine is visible off to the right.

0.5   Go straight ahead on the doubletrack where another road crosses from right to left. The trail veers right out of the meadow and becomes singletrack.

1.4   Pedal smooth tread into Munoz Meadows, a fine series of alpine meadows.

1.9   A singletrack (Dark Hollow Trail) merges from the right; continue straight ahead. Use caution for a steep rocky section right at the end of the meadow.

2.1   The trail starts to descend through aspen stands; hang on for a few steep sections.

2.9   Bear left at the signed junction with the Hendrickson Lake Trail.

3.7   Hendrickson Lake is visible on the left. Turn right at the trail junction (the left trail deadends at the lake).

3.8   Turn left at a signed junction. The smooth singletrack traverses along the aspen-covered hillside.

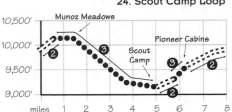

24. Scout Camp Loop

5.0 Pedal into a broad meadow at the Thunder Ridge Boy Scout Camp. Turn left at the sign and follow the doubletrack along the left (east) side of the meadow.

5.3 Turn left at a junction near the headquarters building and follow the doubletrack through the campground.

5.7 Pass through an open gate. The trail becomes rocky, steep singletrack.

6.3 Turn left at an unsigned junction in Pioneer Cabin Meadow. The cabins are off to the left. Follow the singletrack uphill across the meadow. Once in the trees, the trail becomes doubletrack (an old jeep trail) and climbs more steeply. It soon levels off as it passes a couple of small lakes.

7.4 Enter a subdivision. The roads are confusing; generally bear left and downhill.

7.9 Trailhead at the road forks.

Town Loop

Location: In Brian Head.

Distance: 4.2-mile loop.

Time: 1 hour.

Tread: 2.5 miles on wide singletrack; 1.7 miles on paved road.

Aerobic level: Moderate.

Technical difficulty: 2 on singletrack; 1 on pavement.

Hazards: Several street and ATV trail crossings; traffic on Utah Highway 143.

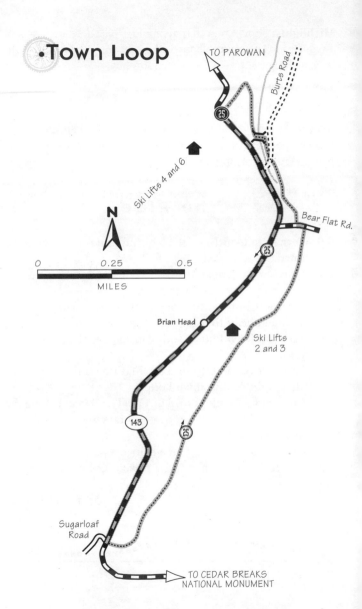

•Town Loop

TO PAROWAN

Burts Road

25

Ski Lifts 4 and 6

Bear Flat Rd.

25

N

| 0 | 0.25 | 0.5 |

MILES

Brian Head

Ski Lifts 2 and 3

143

25

Sugarloaf Road

TO CEDAR BREAKS NATIONAL MONUMENT

Highlights: Short, smooth trail provides bike access to most of Brian Head. The town plans to add a section west of the highway, making the trail a complete loop.

Land status: Private.

Maps: USGS Brian Head.

Access: The north trailhead is 0.1 mile south of Hunter Ridge Road at the north end of town. Park near the highway or in the Navajo Lodge parking lot.

The Ride

0.0 Turn right (south) on the highway and ride through the town.

1.7 Opposite Sugarloaf Road, turn left and descend into the forest on the wide singletrack.

2.1 Turn left onto a dirt road. When the road ends, go straight ahead to regain the wide singletrack.

2.8 Pedal under ski lifts 2 and 3, just above the base buildings.

3.1 Turn left (downhill) on Bear Flat Road, then immediately right on the Town Loop.

3.4 Cross Burts Road, a broad dirt road, and pedal along the left side. The Town Loop soon branches left and goes into the forest.

3.7 Cross Parowan Creek on a bridge.

4.2 The Town Loop ends at the Navajo Lodge parking lot.

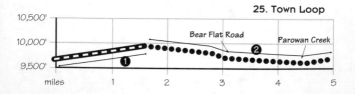

Dark Hollow

Location: 4.8 miles south of Brian Head.

Distance: 15.6 miles one way (shuttle required).

Time: 2 hours.

Tread: 4.9 miles on singletrack; 6.5 miles on doubletrack; 4.2 miles on paved road.

Aerobic level: Moderate.

Technical difficulty: 3 with sections of 4 on singletrack; 2+ on doubletrack; 1 on paved road.

Hazards: Short, steep rocky sections; traffic on highway.

Highlights: A mile-long vertical descent with fun singletrack that starts at timberline and winds through alpine meadows. The lower section is an easy doubletrack cruise through red rock canyons.

Land status: Dixie National Forest.

Maps: USGS Brian Head, Parowan; Dixie National Forest Trails (#702) Illustrated; Dixie National Forest (Pine Valley and Cedar City ranger districts).

Access: First, arrange your shuttle. From the turnoff to the mall in the center of Brian Head, drive about 12 miles north on Utah Highway 143 to Parowan. Turn left at the stop sign and drive two blocks to the Chevron station. Leave the shuttle vehicle here. Then drive back to Brian Head and continue 2.8 miles south on UT 143. Turn left (east) on the Brian Head Peak Road,

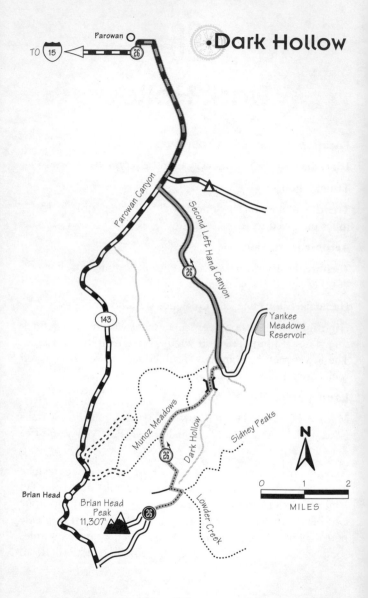

•Dark Hollow

which is maintained dirt. Go 2 miles farther, then park in the trailhead parking lot on the left.

The Ride

0.0 Cross the road to the signed start of the Sidney Peaks Trail, then climb a short, steep switchback onto the ridge. Descend gently along the ridge.

1.0 Turn left onto the Dark Hollow Trail, and roll down a couple of switchbacks. At the bottom, a trail merges from the left. Pedal through several meadows and past tiny Cub Lake. The trail now descends more steeply; use caution for several rocky sections.

2.8 Cruise into Munoz Meadows; the Scout Camp Loop trail merges from the left. Watch your speed at the north end of the meadow—there's a steep rocky pitch right where the trail enters the trees.

3.8 Turn right on the Dark Hollow/Paradise Spring Trail. A short climb leads to a cruise down a gentle ridge through aspens, and then into several narrow switchbacks.

4.9 Cross Dark Hollow Creek on a bridge, then climb over a ridge.

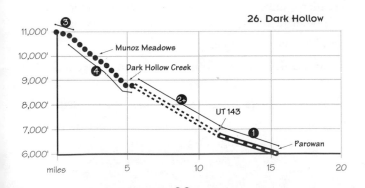

26. Dark Hollow

99

5.6 The trail dives onto Second Left Hand Canyon Road—watch for vehicles. Turn left and descend the spectacular red rock canyon. The road is rough in places and sometimes has washouts.

11.4 The dirt road ends at UT 143. Turn right and roll down the broad asphalt trail to Parowan.

15.4 Turn left at the stop sign.

15.6 The Chevron station on the corner is the normal shuttle pickup, and the end of the ride.

Left Fork Bunker Creek

Location: 4.8 miles south of Brian Head.

Distance: 11.8 miles one way (shuttle required).

Time: 2 hours.

Tread: 6.6 miles on singletrack; 3.8 miles on doubletrack; 0.5 mile on maintained dirt road; 0.9 mile on paved road.

Aerobic level: Moderate.

Technical difficulty: 3 with spots of 3+ on singletrack; 2 on doubletrack and maintained dirt; 1 on paved road.

Hazards: Singletrack section has short, steep, loose descents.

Highlights: Spectacular views from 11,000-foot alpine ridge; great singletrack through fir-aspen forest.

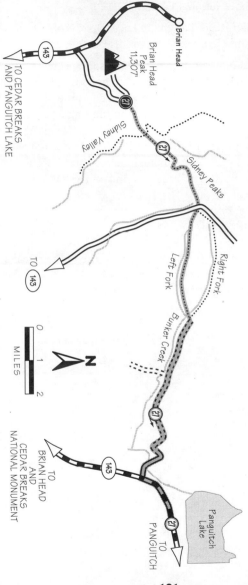

Left Fork Bunker Creek

Brian Head

Brian Head Peak
11,307'

Sidney Valley

Sidney Peaks

Left Fork

Right Fork

Bunker Creek

Panguitch Lake

143

TO CEDAR BREAKS
AND PANGUITCH LAKE

TO 143

143

TO
BRIAN HEAD
AND
CEDAR BREAKS
NATIONAL MONUMENT

TO
PANGUITCH

27

N

MILES
0 1 2

Land status: Dixie National Forest.

Maps: USGS Brian Head, Panguitch Lake; Dixie National Forest (Pine Valley and Cedar City ranger districts).

Access: First, arrange a shuttle by driving south 4 miles from Brian Head on Utah Highway 143. Where UT 148 goes straight, turn left to stay on UT 143 and continue about 14 miles to the Panguitch General Store on the right. Leave the shuttle vehicle here and drive back toward Brian Head. About 1.2 miles past the junction with UT 148, turn right (east) onto Brian Head Peak Road, which is maintained dirt. Go 2 miles farther, then park in the trailhead parking on the left.

The Ride

0.0 Cross the road to the signed start of the Sidney Peaks Trail, then climb a short, steep switchback onto the ridge. Descend gently along the ridge.

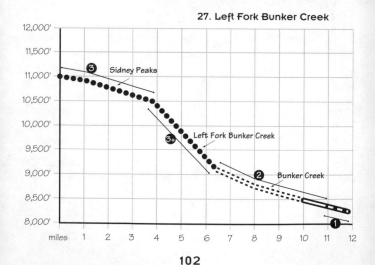

27. Left Fork Bunker Creek

1.0 Ride straight ahead at a signed junction with the Dark Hollow Trail, continuing on the Sidney Peaks Trail, which descends gradually along the ridge. Several faint single and doubletracks merge; stay on the main, well-used singletrack. After passing the Sidney Peaks on the right (southeast), coast down a steep section with numerous roots, then across a nearly level ridge.

3.6 Cruise into a saddle. A sign points back the way you came, along the Sidney Peaks Trail. Stop here and walk out to the overlook, a rock outcrop with fine views to the northwest. Back on your bike, follow the trail across Sidney Valley Road, then turn right onto the Left Fork Bunker Creek Trail. Pedal down a great section of singletrack through aspen and fir forest. The trail always stays just left of the creek. Watch for short, steep, loose sections.

6.6 The singletrack ends at Right Fork Bunker Creek Trailhead. Turn right and pedal down the doubletrack along Bunker Creek.

7.9 Go sharply left at a fork and start climbing for about 0.5 mile.

9.8 Pedal into the Blue Spring Valley.

10.4 The road becomes maintained dirt. Cross the bridge across Blue Spring Creek and climb about 0.3 mile to the highway.

10.9 Turn left (north) on UT 143 and coast 0.9 mile to the Panguitch Lake General Store (the shuttle pickup), on the right just past the Forest Service Campground.

11.8 Panguitch Lake General Store.

Lowder Ponds

Location: 4.8 miles south of Brian Head.

Distance: 10.8-mile loop.

Time: 3 hours.

Tread: 2.7 miles on maintained dirt road; 8.1 miles on singletrack.

Aerobic level: Moderate, with occasional strenuous sections.

Technical difficulty: 3 on singletrack; 2 on maintained dirt road.

Hazards: Watch for short, rocky sections that appear after long smooth stretches of trail; keep your speed down.

Highlights: High alpine ridge at timberline with 100-mile views.

Maps: USGS Brian Head; Dixie National Forest (Pine Valley and Cedar City ranger districts).

Access: From the turnoff to the mall in the center of Brian Head, drive 2.8 miles south on Utah Highway 143, then turn left (east) on Brian Head Peak Road, which is maintained dirt.

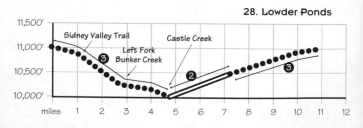

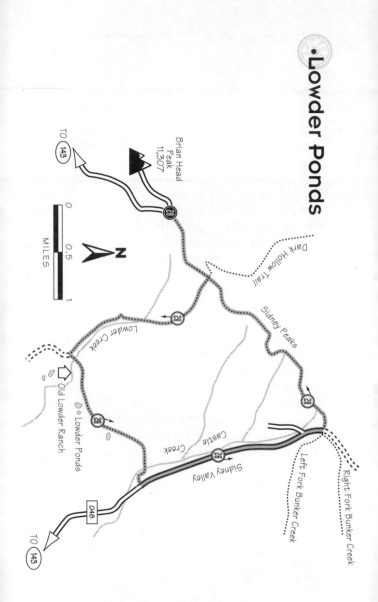

Lowder Ponds

Brian Head Peak 11,307

TO 143

Dark Hollow Trail

Sidney Peaks

Lowder Creek

N

MILES
0   0.5   1

Old Lowder Ranch

Lowder Ponds

Castle Creek

Sidney Valley

048

TO 143

Left Fork Bunker Creek

Right Fork Bunker Creek

Go 2 miles farther, then park in the trailhead parking on the left.

The Ride

0.0 Cross the road to the signed start of the Sidney Peaks Trail, then climb a short, steep switchback onto the ridge. Descend gently along the ridge.

1.0 Turn right at a signed junction onto the Sidney Valley Trail, which descends south away from the ridge. Cross an old road, continuing straight ahead, downhill, on the singletrack. The trail continues its gentle descent through fine alpine meadows and small patches of forest.

2.8 Turn left on a doubletrack road just past a small pond.

2.9 Turn right, downhill, on doubletrack.

3.0 Turn sharply left on faint singletrack near an ancient, gnarled aspen. Before continuing, you may want to ride a few yards to the right to visit the ruins of the Lowder Ranch. After the old aspen, cross a flat meadow; the Lowder Ponds are visible to the right.

3.4 Short, steep climb. A couple of ATV trails merge from the right.

3.9 Enter a meadow, then turn left on a faint singletrack (don't follow the cairned route that continues straight). The singletrack becomes clearer after a few yards as it crosses the meadow. This section ends with a moderate to steep descent into Sidney Valley.

4.7 Cross Castle Creek then climb a short, steep hill to the Sidney Valley Road, which is maintained dirt. Turn left (north) and follow the road as it climbs gently along the expansive meadow.

7.1 A logging road goes left, continue straight on the Sidney Valley Road.

7.4 The road reaches a pass at the head of Sidney Valley. Turn left on the signed Sidney Peaks Trail, which is singletrack. Before continuing, leave your bike and walk a few yards to the overlook, a rock outcrop with a spectacular view of the Parowan Canyon area and the desert ranges to the northwest. The Sidney Peaks Trail climbs around the south side of the Sidney Peaks, alternating gentle and steep climbs.

9.2 Faint singletrack forks left; stay right, along the ridge.

9.8 Close the loop at the junction of the Dark Hollow and Sidney Valley trails. Continue straight on the Sidney Peaks Trail as it climbs gently along the ridge.

10.8 Trailhead on the Brian Head Peak Road.

Dead Lake

Location: About 9 miles southeast of Brian Head.

Distance: 7.4 miles out and back.

Time: 1.5 hours.

Tread: 3.6 miles on doubletrack; 3.8 miles on maintained dirt road.

Aerobic level: Moderate.

Technical difficulty: 2+ on doubletrack; 1 on maintained dirt road.

Hazards: MUD—avoid this ride after a rain!

Highlights: Easy out-and-back ride, with a lake at the end. The

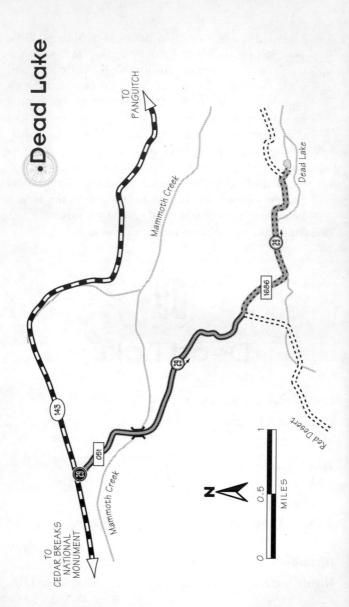

Dead Lake

TO PANGUITCH

Mammoth Creek

Mammoth Creek

143

O51

Dead Lake

1686

Red Desert

TO
CEDAR BREAKS
NATIONAL
MONUMENT

N

0   0.5   1
MILES

fun doubletrack section goes through alpine meadows and has sections with large dips, rocks, and roots that are a good place to hone skills, thanks to a gentle gradient.

Land status: Dixie National Forest.

Maps: USGS Panguitch Lake; Dixie National Forest (#702) Trails Illustrated; Dixie National Forest (Pine Valley and Cedar City ranger districts).

Access: From Brian Head, drive south about 4 miles on Utah Highway 143 to a junction with UT 148. Turn left (east) to stay on UT 143. Go 5 miles, then park at the signed junction with the Red Desert–Tippets Valley Road (Forest Road 051).

The Ride

0.0 Ride the maintained dirt road south across Mammoth Creek on a bridge, then into the aspen-fir forest. It descends gently, but watch for sudden ruts caused by washouts.

1.9 Turn left (southeast) onto the Dead Lake Road (FR 1686), a doubletrack jeep trail. Cross a cattleguard after a short distance, then the road winds through meadows beside a small creek. Roller-coaster sections of deep potholes (hopefully dry) make part of the track a fun obstacle course.

3.6 After a short, steep downhill section, turn right at an unsigned junction and pedal the last few yards to the lake.

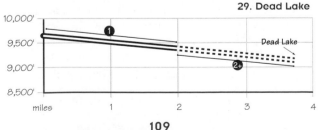

29. Dead Lake

3.7 Dead Lake is shallow but has a reputation for fine trout fishing. This is the end of the ride; retrace your tracks from here.

Red Desert Loop

Location: About 11 miles southeast of Brian Head.

Distance: 13.3-mile loop.

Time: 2.5 hours.

Tread: 8.6 miles on doubletrack; 4.7 miles on maintained dirt road.

Aerobic level: Moderate.

Technical difficulty: 2 and 2+ on doubletrack; 1 on dirt road.

Hazards: Deep, sticky, bike-engulfing mud. Don't even think of doing this ride after a rain!

Highlights: Loop ride with minor elevation change, through scenic meadows and aspen groves.

Land status: Dixie National Forest.

Maps: USGS Panguitch Lake, Henrie Knolls; Dixie National Forest (Pine Valley and Cedar City ranger districts).

Access: From Brian Head, drive south about 4 miles on Utah Highway 143 to the junction with UT 148. Turn left (east) to stay on UT 143. Go 5 miles, then turn right (south) on the signed Red Desert–Tippets Valley Road (Forest Road 051). Drive 2.3 miles on this maintained dirt road and park where the

•Red Desert Loop

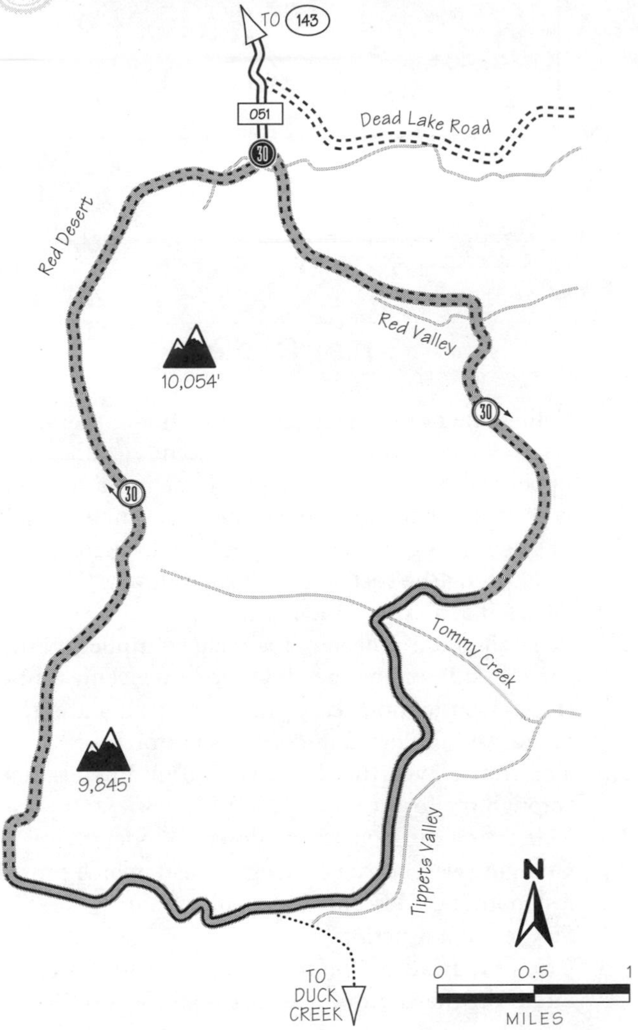

TO (143)

051

(30)

Dead Lake Road

Red Desert

Red Valley

10,054'

(30)

(30)

Tommy Creek

9,845'

Tippets Valley

TO
DUCK
CREEK

N

0   0.5   1
MILES

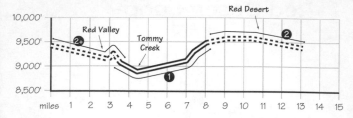

Red Valley jeep trail forks left. (Don't confuse this jeep trail with the Dead Lake Road, 0.4 mile north).

The Ride

0.0 Follow the doubletrack jeep trail left (southeast) as it starts a gradual climb. Soon, it descends gently into the upper end of Red Valley, a fine alpine meadow fringed with aspen. The old road becomes faint in the meadow but stays along the left side. You'll pedal across a small creek along the east side of this meadow.

1.9 Turn left at a faint T intersection.

2.0 Pedal right onto the faint road that continues to follow the left side of the meadow. Don't descend into the trees. After a short, easy climb, the trail starts to descend, and the meadow becomes narrower.

3.0 The trail leaves the drainage and climbs gradually through the forest.

3.4 Ride over a cattleguard and down a moderate hill.

3.7 Go right (west) on a new logging road, which provides a smooth, fast descent to the valley floor.

4.1 Stay left at a junction.

4.5 Cross the head of Tommy Creek, and start a gradual climb on the maintained dirt road. Several logging roads branch right in the next mile; ignore them all. After a while, you'll ride into the open expanse of Tippets Valley.

6.7 Go straight where a signed jeep trail goes left to Duck Creek. Now the road starts to climb, but the grade is never severe.

7.1 The grade moderates as the road passes through several meadows.

8.4 Pedal right (north) onto the Red Desert Road, which starts out maintained dirt but quickly becomes doubletrack. (This junction is signed for Tippets Valley and Sage Valley but not for Red Desert.)

9.4 The road becomes rough and rocky as it descends slightly to avoid an impassable lava flow on the plateau.

10.4 Ride into the south end of Red Desert, a long, semi-circular sage valley that is not red at all. The road soon levels out and then starts a gradual descent.

13.3 The ride ends at the junction with the Red Valley jeep trail.

Thunder Mountain Trail

Location: About 65 miles east of Cedar City.

Distance: 14.8-mile loop.

Time: 3 hours.

Tread: 5 miles on paved road; 2.2 miles on doubletrack; 7.6 miles on singletrack.

Aerobic level: Moderate.

Technical difficulty: 3 with sections of 4+ on singletrack; 2 on doubletrack; 1 on paved road.

Hazards: Heavy traffic on highway, dropoffs near trail, and loose, rocky sections on singletrack.

Highlights: The trails in Bryce Canyon National Park are closed to bikes, but this great ride descends singletrack through hoodoo country very much like that found in the park.

Land status: Dixie National Forest.

Maps: USGS Wilson Peak; Dixie National Forest (Powell, Escalante, and Teasdale ranger districts).

Access: From the junction of U.S. Highway 89 and Utah Highway 12, drive 2 miles east on UT 12 and park at the signed Thunder Mountain Trailhead, on the right just as the road enters Red Canyon.

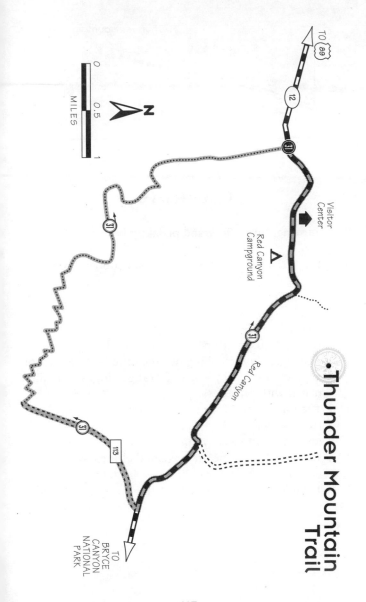

·Thunder Mountain Trail

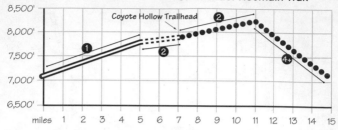

31. Thunder Mountain Trail

The Ride

0.0   Turn right on UT 12 and pedal up beautiful Red Canyon.

5.0   Leave the pavement for a dirt road (Forest Road 113) on the right (south) signed for the Fremont Trail.

5.8   Go straight to Coyote Hollow Trailhead.

7.2   Coyote Hollow Trailhead; pedal up a short hill to start on the Thunder Mountain Trail. It winds around orange ridges dotted with ponderosa pine, descending into drainages then climbing out the other side. Soon you are surrounded by a sea of orange ridges—an alien planet with pine trees.

11.1   The high point of the trail. It starts to descend along a ridge; sections are loose and rocky. A series of switchbacks drops you into a canyon.

13.4   The trail leaves the drainage and climbs over a small pass; it's a gentle downhill cruise from here.

14.8   Thunder Mountain Trailhead and the end of the ride.

32

Cassidy Trail

Location: About 67 miles east of Cedar City.

Distance: 16.7-mile loop.

Time: 4 hours.

Tread: 1.9 miles on paved highway; 6.6 miles on doubletrack road; 8.2 miles on singletrack.

Aerobic level: Strenuous.

Technical difficulty: 3 with some 4 on singletrack; 2 on doubletrack; 1 on paved highway.

Hazards: Heavy tourist traffic on highway; horses and hikers on singletrack, especially last 2 miles.

Highlights: Scenic loop through orange limestone canyons, on a trail supposedly used by the famous outlaw Butch Cassidy.

Land status: Dixie National Forest.

Maps: USGS Wilson Peak, Casto Canyon; Dixie National Forest (#705) Trails Illustrated; Dixie National Forest (Powell, Escalante, and Teasdale ranger districts).

Access: From the junction of U.S. Highway 89 and Utah Highway 12, drive 4.5 miles east on UT 12 and turn left into the Red Canyon Trailhead. (You'll pass the Forest Service Visitor Center, which has water, maps, and trail information.)

•Cassidy Trail

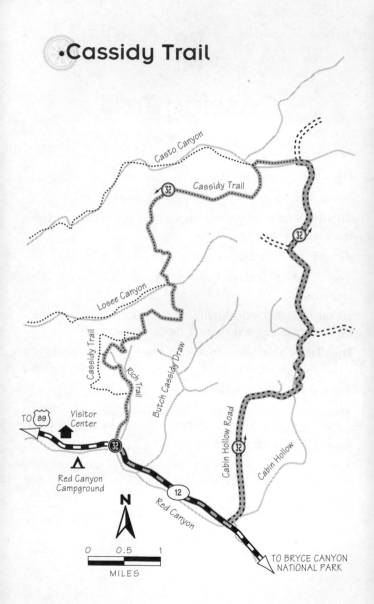

The Ride

0.0   Leave your vehicle at Red Canyon Trailhead and turn left onto UT 12 for an easy climb up scenic Red Canyon. Use caution at the two short but narrow tunnels.

1.9   Pedal left (north) onto Cabin Hollow Road (Forest Road 120). The road winds up a shallow canyon.

5.7   Go left on FR 121. Notice the change from orange-pink to gray rock. This area is covered with dark volcanic rocks, which means mud after a rain!

6.8   Cross a pass with panoramic views and coast into Casto Canyon.

6.9   Straight at a junction with another doubletrack.

8.3   Lean left at a junction.

8.5   Go left (downhill) to start Casto Canyon Trail, which is singletrack.

9.0   Left onto Cassidy Trail, which climbs out of the canyon in a series of short, steep climbs.

10.5 Ride straight ahead at a junction with an unsigned singletrack. The trail works its way around the north and west sides of a hill, with a lot of up and down.

11.7 Ride through Little Desert, a small badlands, and then descend into Losee Canyon.

12.6 Cross the Losee Canyon Trail at the bottom of Losee Canyon, and climb (Ugh! Steep!) onto a neat little plateau dotted with stately ponderosa pines.

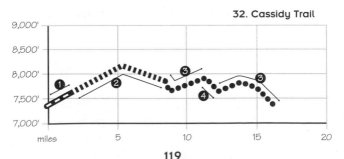

32. Cassidy Trail

14.1 Go left (south) at a junction, staying with the Cassidy Trail.

14.4 Turn left on the Rich Trail (you can follow the Cassidy Trail through this section, if desired—it's about 0.5 mile longer). The trail traverses along the hillside, then starts to drop into the canyon below.

14.9 Turn left onto the Cassidy Trail, then after a few yards go left again on the Cassidy Trail.

15.9 Go left at another junction. Cruise down the canyon bottom, but watch for hikers.

16.7 Red Canyon Trailhead and the end of the ride.

Sunset Cliffs

Location: About 80 miles east of Cedar City.

Distance: 17.7-mile loop.

Time: 3 hours.

Tread: 1.6 miles on maintained dirt; 16.1 miles on doubletrack.

Aerobic level: Moderate.

Technical difficulty: 2 on doubletrack; 1 on maintained dirt road.

Hazards: Occasional washouts on doubletrack; vehicle traffic.

Highlights: Scenic loop with views from the Sunset Cliffs.

Land status: Dixie National Forest.

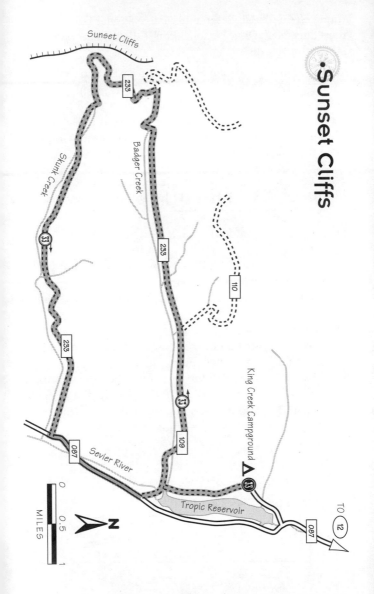

Sunset Cliffs

Maps: USGS Tropic Reservoir; Dixie National Forest (#705) Trails Illustrated; Dixie National Forest (Powell, Escalante, and Teasdale ranger districts).

Access: From the junction of U.S. Highway 89 and Utah Highway 12, drive east about 11 miles on UT 12, then turn right (south) on the Tropic Reservoir Road (Forest Road 087). Follow this maintained dirt road 7.2 miles, then turn right (west) on the signed road to King Creek Campground. Continue about 0.5 mile and park at the campground.

The Ride

- **0.0** Go south on a doubletrack along the west side of the lake.
- **1.3** Turn right (west) on FR 109 and ride up Badger Creek. The doubletrack climbs steadily.
- **3.5** Pedal straight ahead on FR 233, still following Badger Creek.
- **5.0** The road becomes steeper.
- **7.1** Go left (south) on FR 233; the road levels out and follows the edge of the Sunset Cliffs.
- **8.7** Walk a few yards off the road and enjoy the view from the Sunset Cliffs. You'll see the white cliffs of Zion National Park and the high plateau near Brian Head. Then follow the road as it descends Skunk Creek.

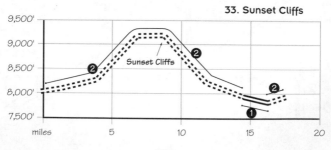

33. Sunset Cliffs

12.0 The road levels out and emerges in a meadow.
14.5 Turn left (north) on FR 087, a maintained dirt road.
16.1 Pedal left (west) on FR 109, Badger Creek Road.
16.4 Turn right (north) and follow the doubletrack along the west side of Tropic Reservoir.
17.7 King Creek Campground and the end of the ride.

Pink Cliffs

Location: About 90 miles east of Cedar City.

Distance: 13.3-mile loop.

Time: 2 hours.

Tread: 6 miles on doubletrack; 7.3 miles on maintained dirt road.

Aerobic level: Moderate.

Technical difficulty: 2 on doubletrack; 1 on dirt roads.

Hazards: Occasional traffic on road.

Highlights: This is a road cruise well suited to beginner and intermediate riders, but everyone will enjoy the scenic views of the Pink Cliffs.

Land status: Dixie National Forest.

Maps: USGS Podunk Creek; Dixie National Forest (Powell, Escalante, and Teasdale ranger districts).

Access: From Cedar City, drive east 42 miles on Utah Highway 14, then turn left on U.S. Highway 89. Drive 20 miles and turn

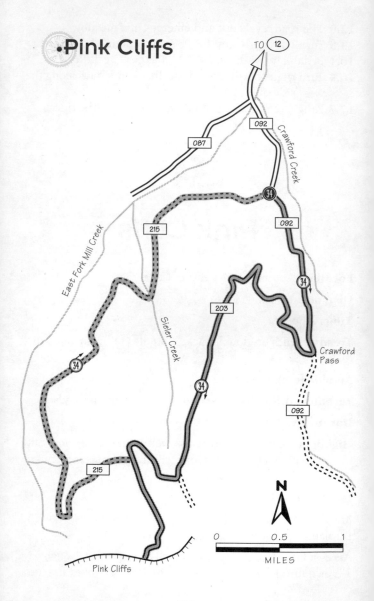

•Pink Cliffs

TO 12

092
087
Crawford Creek

34

215
092

34

203

34

East Fork Mill Creek

Sieler Creek

34

Crawford Pass

092

215

34

N

0   0.5   1
MILES

Pink Cliffs

124

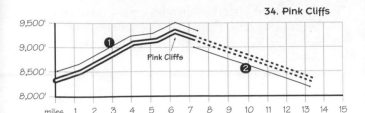

right on UT 12. After about 11 miles, turn right on the Tropic Reservoir road (Forest Road 087). Continue 18 miles on this maintained dirt road, then turn left onto the road to Crawford Pass (FR 092). Go 1.1 miles, and park at the signed junction with the Pink Cliffs Road (FR 215).

The Ride

0.0 Pedal up the left-hand road (the right fork will be your return). The maintained road climbs steadily above Crawford Creek.

1.5 At Crawford Pass, turn right onto FR 203. The climb becomes somewhat steeper, but moderates just as the rim of the Pink Cliffs comes into view, providing scenic as well as physical relief.

4.1 Turn right (uphill) on FR 215.

5.2 Turn left (south) at the sign for the Pink Cliffs. This maintained but somewhat cobbly road climbs to the overlook. When you reach the rim, pedal right along a short singletrack to the actual overlook.

6.3 This is the southernmost point of the Paunsaugunt Plateau. The view includes Zion National Park to the west, Arizona's Kaibab Plateau to the south, and the blue dome of Navajo Mountain to the southeast. After soaking up the view, coast back down the road.

7.3 Turn left on FR 215, which becomes a doubletrack. It's mostly downhill cruising through alpine forest, with a few short easy climbs, all the way back to the starting point.

13.3 End of the ride.

Powell Point

Location: About 97 miles east of Cedar City.

Distance: 9 miles out and back.

Time: 1 hour.

Tread: 7.4 miles on doubletrack; 1.6 miles on singletrack.

Aerobic level: Easy.

Technical difficulty: 2 on doubletrack and singletrack.

Hazards: The ride is on a high, exposed ridge; don't be out here during late summer thunderstorms!

Highlights: Scenic ridge on the highest plateau in North America. Views east and west along the ride, culminating in a 270-degree panorama at Powell Point.

Land status: Dixie National Forest.

Maps: USGS Pine Lake; Dixie National Forest (Powell, Escalante, and Teasdale ranger districts).

Access: From the junction of U.S. Highway 89 and Utah Highway 12, drive 13 miles east on UT 12, then turn north on UT 22. Go about 11 miles, then turn right on the signed road

•Powell Point

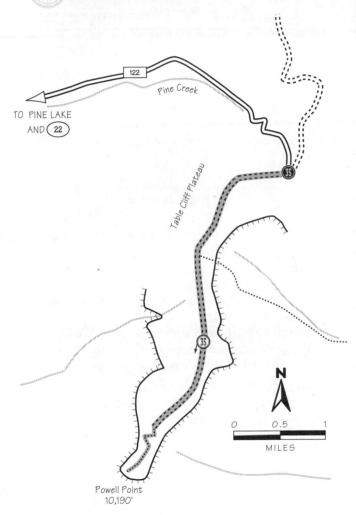

122

Pine Creek

TO PINE LAKE
AND 22

Table Cliff Plateau

35

35

Powell Point
10,190'

N

0   0.5   1

MILES

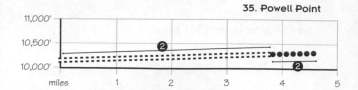

to Pine Lake (Forest Road 122). This road is passable for any vehicle as far as Pine Lake; a high-clearance vehicle is needed for the last 6.3 miles. Continue 11 miles to the top of the plateau. An unmarked jeep road branches right (south) just as the main road swings north. Drive a few more yards and park at the viewpoint.

The Ride

0.0 Pedal (right) up the jeep trail that climbs and descends over several gentle hills. After passing a meadow, the ridge narrows and there are occasional views.

3.7 The road ends; ride the nice little section of singletrack out to the point. The trail drops into a saddle then climbs to the end.

4.5 Powell Point, named after Major John Wesley Powell, the government scientist who put this region on the map in the 1870s. Ride back the way you came.

Option: You could ride from Pine Lake if you want to make it a longer, strenuous effort—this adds 12.6 miles round trip, and 1,800 feet of climbing to the ride.

Appendix

Information Sources

LAND MANAGEMENT OFFICES

Bureau of Land Management
Arizona Strip District Office
345 E. Riverside Dr.
St. George, UT 84770
(435) 688-3200

Cedar City District Office
176 E. D.L. Sargent Dr.
Cedar City, UT 84720
(435) 586-2401

National Park Service
Bryce Canyon National Park
P.O. Box 170001
Bryce Canyon, Utah 84717-0001
(435) 834-5322

Cedar Breaks National Monument
82 N. 100 East, Suite 3
Cedar City, UT 84720
(435) 586-9451

Zion National Park
Springdale, UT 84767-1099
(435) 722-3256

USDA Forest Service (Dixie National Forest)
Supervisor's Office
82 N. 100 West
Cedar City, UT 84720
(435) 865-3700

Cedar City Ranger District
82 N. 100 East
Cedar City, UT 84720
(435) 865-3200

Escalante Ranger District
755 West Main
P.O. Box 246
Escalante, UT 84726
(435) 826-5400

Pine Valley Ranger District
196 E. Tabernacle Dr.
St. George, UT 84770
(435) 652-3200

Powell Ranger District
225 E. Center
P.O. Box 80
Panguitch, UT 84759
(435) 676-8815

Utah State Division of Wildlife Resources
Southern Region Office
1470 North Airport Road
Cedar City, UT 84720
(435) 865-6100

BIKE SHOPS

St. George

Bicycles Unlimited
90 South 100 East
St. George, UT 84770
(435) 673-4492
(888) 673-4492

Red Rock Bicycle
190 S. Main
St. George, UT 84770
(435) 674-3185

Springdale (Zion National Park)

Bike Zion
1478 Zion Park Blvd.
Springdale, UT 84767
(800) 4-SLIKROK
(435) 772-3929
(435) 619-A-RIDE (cell)
(435) 635-4065 (home)

Scenic Cycles
205 Zion Park Blvd.
Springdale, UT 84767
(435) 772-2453

Cedar City

Bike Route
70 W. Center
Cedar City, UT 84720
(435) 586-4242

Cedar Cycle
38 E. 200 South
Cedar City, UT 84720
(435) 586-5210

Brian Head

Brian Head Cross Country and Bike
The Lodge at Brian Head
314 Hunter Ridge Dr.
P.O. Box 190065
Brian Head, UT 84719
(435) 677-2012

Brianhead Sports
269 S. Brian Head Blvd.
P.O. Box 190277
Brian Head, UT 84719
(435) 677-2014

Georg's Ski Shop
612 S. Highway 43
P.O. Box 190183
Brian Head, UT 84719
(435) 677-2013

Bryce Area

Mountain Bike Heaven
25 E. Center St.
P.O. Box 592
Panguitch, UT 84759
(435) 676-2880

Ruby's Inn
South Highway 63
Bryce, UT 86764
(435) 834-5341

Glossary

ATB: All-terrain bicycle; a.k.a. mountain bike, sprocket rocket, fat-tire flyer.

ATV: All-terrain vehicle; in this book ATV refers to motorbikes and three- or four-wheelers designed for off-road use.

Bail: Getting off the bike, usually in a hurry, whether or not you meant to. Often a last resort. Also, to end a ride early. "We ran out of water early and had to bail."

Bunny hop: Leaping up, while riding, and lifting both wheels off the ground to jump over an obstacle (or for sheer joy).

Butt ruff: A rocky trail that pounds the rider through the saddle, especially on descent. Will this term become obsolete with the spread of fully suspended bikes?

Cherry stem: The out-and-back section of a ride, the rest of which is a loop.

Clean: To ride without touching a foot (or other body part) to the ground; to ride a tough section successfully.

Clipless pedal: A type of pedal with a binding that accepts a matching cleat on the sole of a bike shoe. The cleat locks to the pedal for more control and efficient pedaling, and is easily unlatched for safe landings (in theory). Also known as "spuds."

Contour: A line on a topographic map showing a continuous elevation level over uneven ground.

Dab: To put a foot or a hand down (or to hold onto or lean on a tree or other support) while riding. If you have to dab, then you haven't ridden that piece of trail clean.

Downfall: Trees and mountain bikers that have fallen across the track (also deadfall).

Doubletrack: A trail, jeep road, ATV route, or other track with two distinct ribbons of tread, typically with grass growing in between. No matter which side you choose, the other rut always looks smoother.

Endo: Lifting the rear wheel off the ground and riding (or abruptly not riding) on the front wheel only. Also known, at various degrees of control and finality, as a nose wheelie, going over the handlebars, and a face plant.

Fall line: The angle and direction of a slope; the line you follow when gravity is in control and you aren't.

Graded: When a gravel road is scraped smooth to level out the washboards and potholes, it has been graded. In this book, a road is listed as graded only if it is regularly maintained. Even these roads are not always graded every year.

Granny gear: The combination of gears that provides your easiest gear ratio, used for climbing steep sections. Shift to the innermost and smallest of the chainrings on the bottom bracket spindle (where the pedals and crank arms attach to the bike's frame) and up to the biggest cog on the rear hub to find your granny gear.

Hammer: To ride hard; derived from how it feels afterward: "I'm hammered."

Hammerhead: Someone who actually enjoys feeling hammered. A Type-A rider who goes hard and fast all the time.

Kelly hump: An abrupt mound of dirt across the road or trail. These are common on old logging roads and skidder tracks, placed there to block vehicle access. At high speeds, they become launching pads that transform bikes into satellites and riders into astronauts.

Line: The route (or trajectory) between or over obstacles or through turns. Tread, or trail, refers to the ground you're riding on; the *line* is the path you choose within the tread (and exists mostly in the eye of the beholder).

Off-the-seat: Moving your butt behind the bike seat and over the rear tire; used for control on extremely steep descents. This position increases braking power, helps prevent endos, and reduces skidding.

Portage: To carry the bike, usually up a steep hill, across unrideable zobstacles, or through a stream.

Quads: Thigh muscles (short for quadriceps); or maps in the USGS topographic series (short for quadrangles). The right quads (of either kind) can prevent or get you out of trouble in the backcountry.

Racheting: Also known as backpedaling; pedaling backwards to avoid bashing feet or pedals on rocks or other obstacles.

Sidehill: Where the trail crosses a slope's fall line. If the tread is narrow, keep your uphill pedal up to avoid hitting the ground. If the tread has a sideways slant, you may have to use body English to keep the bike vertical and avoid side-slipping.

Singletrack: A trail, game run, or other track with only one ribbon of tread. But this is like defining an orgasm as a muscle cramp. Good singletrack is pure fun.

Spur: A side road or trail that splits off from the main route.

Surf: Riding through loose gravel or sand, when the wheels slalom from side to side. Also *heavy surf*: frequent and difficult obstacles.

Suspension: A bike with front suspension has a shock-absorbing fork or stem. Rear suspension absorbs shock between the rear wheel and frame. A bike with both is said to be fully suspended.

Switchbacks: When a trail goes up a steep slope, it zigzags or *switchbacks* across the fall line to ease the gradient of the climb. Well-designed switchbacks make a turn with at least an eight-foot radius and remain fairly level within the turn itself. These are rare, however, and cyclists often struggle through sharply angled, sloping switchbacks, which were designed for hikers and equestrians.

Track stand: Balancing on a bike in one place, without rolling forward appreciably. Cock the front wheel to one side and bring that pedal up to the 1 or 2 o'clock position. Now control your side-to-side balance by applying pressure on the pedals and brakes and changing the angle of the front wheel, as needed. It takes practice but really comes in handy at stoplights, on switchbacks, and when trying to free a foot before falling (see clipless pedal).

Tread: The riding surface, particularly regarding singletrack.

Water bar: A log, rock, ditch, or other barrier placed in the tread to divert water off the trail and prevent erosion. Be alert for peeled logs, especially those at sharp angles across the trail. They may be slippery, which can result in bad falls.

A Short Index of Rides

Road Rides
16. Cedar Breaks

Beginner's Luck
2. Gunlock Loop (with shuttle)
3. West Canyon
8. Dutchman Trail
23. Pioneer Cabins
25. Town Loop
29. Dead Lake
30. Red Desert Loop

Sweet Singletrack Rides
4. Green Valley Loop
5. Stucki Spring Loop
6. Church Rock Loop
11. J.E.M. Trail
12. Gooseberry Mesa
17. Navajo Lake Loop
18. Cascade Falls Loop (and Virgin River Rim Trail option, see Rides 18, 19, and 20)
20. Strawberry Point Loop
24. Scout Camp Loop
26. Dark Hollow
27. Left Fork Bunker Creek
28. Lowder Ponds
31. Thunder Mountain Trail
32. Cassidy Trail

Slickrock Fun: Petrified Sand Dunes!
6.   Church Rock Loop
12.   Gooseberry Mesa

Technical Tests (If you ain't bleedin', you ain't ridin'!)
4.   Green Valley Loop
6.   Church Rock Loop
12.   Gooseberry Mesa
14.   Red Mountain
15.   Blowhard Mountain
26.   Dark Hollow
27.   Left Fork Bunker Creek
31.   Thunder Mountain Trail
32.   Cassidy Trail

Great Climbs: The Yearn to Burn!
9.   Silver Reef
10.   Oak Grove
21.   Yankee Meadows

Great Downhills: The Need for Speed
26.   Dark Hollow
27.   Left Fork Bunker Creek
28.   Lowder Ponds
31.   Thunder Mountain Trail

About the Author

Bruce Grubbs is an avid hiker, mountain biker, and cross-country skier who has been exploring the American desert for over 30 years. An outdoor writer and photographer, he's written eight other FalconGuides. He lives in Flagstaff, Arizona.